RAILWAYS BETWEEN THE WARS

Glasgow - Oban train, near Glenogle Summit, hauled by McIntosh 0—6—0 No 757 (still in Caledonian livery) and '55' class 460 No 14607, shortly after Grouping. From a painting by Victor Welch

RAILWAYS BETWEEN THE WARS

by H. C. Casserley

David & Charles : Newton Abbot

ISBN 0 7153 5294 6

Set in ten on eleven point Plantin
and printed in Great Britain
by W J Holman Limited Dawlish
for David & Charles (Publishers) Limited
South Devon House Newton Abbot Devon

Contents

Introduction

THE PERIOD between the two world wars, that is, roughly speaking, from 1919 to 1939, covered what was perhaps the most interesting phase of railway history in the United Kingdom. Many in fact claim that the later 1930s saw railways at the peak of their achievement, although some maintain that this description more rightfully belonged to the years immediately prior to the first war. The greatest single event was undoubtedly the grouping which took place on 1 January 1923, as a result of the 1921 Railways Act, under which over a hundred hitherto separate undertakings became merged into four new companies, of which only one, the Great Western, perpetuated the identity of any of the previous main line systems.

The older enthusiasts who still remember vividly the glamorous pre-amalgamation days have now already dwindled to a mere handful, perhaps not much more than two or three dozen at the most, and in not so many years we shall be practically an extinct species—'gone with the wind'.

The memories of the finest part of the post-grouping era are, however, still enjoyed by what may be called the middle-aged section of today's railway devotees and historians, and this book is by its very nature largely concerned with that period.

It is obviously impossible to do more within the confines of one volume than to summarise the more interesting aspects of the passing scene and the various developments and changes which took place. All this has been written and recorded fully in all its various aspects by such well known writers as Cecil J. Allen, O. S. Nock, C. Hamilton Ellis, and many others, and this volume can do little more than to attempt to recall this fascinating period by a general survey, when it is hoped that some new angles of thought now and then, together with the odd personal recollection here and there, may emerge. If the main emphasis is on locomotives and train working, this is because this aspect of railways has always had the widest general appeal.

The principal companies in the period just prior to the grouping together with the four newly created concerns, must inevitably take up the major portion of the book, but the smaller lines and light railways are not entirely neglected. The development of electrification and other forms of motive power likewise forms an important part of the story. There is also a section devoted to the Irish railways, as it must be remembered that in 1919 the whole of Ireland, north and south, was still part of Britain, its railways being not only closely bound to the general British railway system, but in one or two instances under the actual ownership of railways in England.

Space again precludes extended reference to some of the more specialised technical subjects such as signalling, these matters being already covered elsewhere by treatises specifically devoted to them, but a section on coaching stock seems to be justified as being a subject, which although largely neglected in the past, is one in which there have lately been signs of increasing interest.

With such a wide range of possible subjects it is difficult to select the illustrations, which must be chosen with care to represent as far as possible either something representative of each major event, or appertaining to as many railways as possible. The great difficulty is not what to include, but what must be left out. Endeavour has been made to avoid not only too many hackneyed or conventional types of view, but in particular well-known illustrations, and in fact, as far as possible to make use where practicable of hitherto unpublished and unknown photographs.

H. C. CASSERLEY
Berkhamsted, July 1970

Early Years and the 1921 Railways Act

THIS NECESSARILY condensed outline of the principal events which took place during the period under review should, and in fact obviously must, commence with that memorable date, 11 November 1918. I was at school at the time, but remember clearly as if it were yesterday our being assembled in the big hall to hear the Headmaster's solemn announcement: 'At the eleventh hour of the eleventh day of the eleventh month in this year of grace, Germany finally surrendered, and we are no longer at war. Thanks be to God.' It had been a war to end all wars; henceforth mankind would live in peace. How little we knew, or how naïve could we have been at the time! For many years the ceremony of the eleventh of November was perpetuated as a silent memorial to those who gave their lives, and it is worth placing on record that on the first anniversary, 11 November 1919, the two minutes' silence was observed so rigorously that all trains, even the 'Cornish Riviera Express', came to a complete stand during this time.

The four wearying years of exceptional traffic had left the railways in a much run-down condition. Field Marshal Haig paid special tribute to the great contribution they had made in the prosecution of the war, singling out for special mention the South Eastern & Chatham. By its geographical situation it was the very lifeline of communication to the important channel ports of Folkestone, Dover, and the newly created wartime port of Richborough, and had borne the brunt of the extra military traffic to the continent. As if this of itself had not been enough to contend with, there had been a severe landslide at the cliffs overlooking the Warren, between Folkestone and Dover, a notorious trouble spot. This occurred on 19 December 1915, resulting in the complete closure of this vital link until 11 August 1919, with the diversion of all Dover traffic via Canterbury. The LSWR and LB & SCR were similarly affected by virtue of their geographical position as gateways to France and Europe, though to a lesser extent, by the additional military traffic over the New-haven and Southampton routes. Ordinary services to the continent had of course been suspended during the war, but from 3 February 1919 civilian passengers could again travel between London and Paris via Folkestone and Boulogne.

At the other end of the country, the Highland was also a railway which had to carry an enormous additional traffic over its attenuated route—largely single line—owing to the large naval concentration at Scapa Flow, off the far north coast of Scotland.

Most of the companies were eager to restore full passenger facilities, which had been severely curtailed during the emergency. These included the restoration of restaurant facilities, sleeping cars, and so on, coupled with a desire to achieve a quick return to pre-war standards of speed and comfort. By 1920 some railways, notably the Lancashire & Yorkshire, LB & SCR, SE & CR, and the Great Eastern, even found it possible to reintroduce some long-distance excursion facilities, which had of course been amongst the first casualties of wartime austerity. The Great Western had inaugurated cheap day return tickets available by ordinary trains as early as July 1919. These were the days of healthy competition between rival companies, particularly those serving the same towns and areas.

At the same time labour troubles began to arise soon after the Armistice. During the actual period of hostilities railwaymen (and women) of all grades had worked hard and loyally along with the rest of the population in the common cause, but although wages had risen considerably, there was now emerging a clamour for improved conditions, the first achievement being a reduction in hours as from 1 February 1919.

Mr J. H. Thomas, a well-known figure in later years, became secretary of the National Union of Railwaymen. A railway strike commenced on 26

September 1919, but skeleton services were kept going to some extent by loyal railwaymen (who earned for themselves the description of 'black-legs') assisted by volunteers, mainly students, a total and complete walk-out such as occurs nowa-days in any section of industry being unknown at the time.

The exigencies of wartime conditions had re-sulted in many unusual sights in the way of loco-motives far from their native haunts. The High-land in particular suffered from a great shortage of motive power and had to borrow engines from several sources, even the LSWR and LB & SCR. Glasgow & South Western engines were to be seen in London on the GWR, and even as late as 1920 Hull & Barnsley 0-6-0s were to be found on the SE & CR.

Some railways, notably the Midland, Great Western, Caledonian, and North British, provided large numbers, chiefly 0-6-0s, for work on the continent, most of which duly returned and were to be seen at odd times around 1919 passing through London and other centres on their way back to their old systems. All were repaired and put in many years of further service. Robinson's well-known 2-8-0 design for the Great Central was adopted by the War Department as a stan-dard type for overseas use and several hundred were built by outside firms. On being repatriated they were disposed of, some to overseas buyers, and others to railways in this country, the Great Western and LNWR in particular, and many to the LNER, some of these being eventually called up for a second time to serve in World War II.

Standards of maintenance had naturally suffered during World War I to some extent, although to nothing like the deplorable standards of World War II, painting and even cleaning not being entirely neglected. Some lines kept their full liveries right through the conflict, but many adopted simpler and more austere styles of paint-ing, in most cases never to resume their former glories. Amongst these may be mentioned the South Eastern & Chatham, which abandoned its rich green with elaborate lining out in favour of plain grey black, incidentally with large numerals on the tender or tank sides, Midland style. The Great Eastern also went in for plain grey, again with large numerals, in place of its well-known dark blue; grey was also adopted by the Great Northern for all but its express passenger engines, whilst many Great Western engines appeared in a peculiar brownish shade described officially as 'khaki'.

The principal locomotive development in these intermediate years prior to the grouping was un-doubtedly the almost simultaneous introduction in 1922 of the Pacific express engine by the Great Northern and North Eastern Railways, a type hitherto represented by one solitary example, *The Great Bear* of the GWR. Oddly enough, this rail-way never perpetuated the 4-6-2, although the type was later to become the standard large ex-press locomotive on both the LMS and LNER, and eventually on the Southern.

The railways had been taken over by the Government at the outbreak of war in August 1914, but on 13 August 1919 a bill for the crea-tion of a new Ministry of Transport received the royal assent, and control passed to the new organ-isation, which dealt not only with railways, but all forms of transport. Sir Eric Geddes was the first Minister of Transport.

Exactly how far or in what form control over the railways should be exercised in the future was the subject of much discussion and argument. Even at that time the question of nationalisation was seriously considered, but in the event it was to be a further thirty-eight years with another intervening world war before this became an accomplished fact. Some form of amalgamation, however, was deemed necessary, although not per-haps altogether desirable from all points of view. Several schemes were put forward. What event-ually materialised was, of course, the Railways Act of 1921, resulting in the creation of four new companies embodying amalgamations of many of the previously independent lines, large and small, effective as from 1 January 1923.

This was undoubtedly one of the most important events in the railway history of Great Britain.

Various alternative proposals concerning the number and composition of the new groups had been considered. One of them contemplated five divisions instead of four, the fifth comprising all railways within the greater London area, but this proposal was not adopted in the final plan. Metro-politan and associated lines, together with the tubes, were left out of it altogether. (These were to be amalgamated later, in 1933, together with the bus and tramway systems, into a new concern, the London Passenger Transport Board.)

Anyway, the decision was finally in favour of four main groups, the London Midland & Scot-tish, London & North Eastern, Great Western, and Southern. In the case of the Great Western, which alone retained its old title, it was in effect nothing more than the absorption by one large company of a number of smaller ones. The Southern on the other hand had three predominating partners, and the other two several.

It eventually became apparent that the LMS was in practice too large and unwieldy (it was in fact the largest company and railway in the world), and it would have been better if it had been split in some way. One very happy solution would undoubtedly have been to leave the LNWR and L & YR as the principal elements of one group. They had actually anticipated matters by amalgamating a year earlier, on 1 January 1922, though without any outwardly visible effect. For a short space of one year this had become by far the largest railway in the country, with a capital of some two hundred million pounds, one-eighth of the total capital in the UK, a route mileage of 2,667, and over 3,250 locomotives. A much more compact and easily worked group would have been a combination of the Midland and Great Central (which company actually went in with the LNER) which covers much of the same territory.

As an interesting sidelight on this speculation, one wonders whether had things been different, we might have had the sight of GCR engines painted in the lovely Midland red livery, which was adopted by the LMS at first for its passenger engines. Pollitt and Robinson 4-4-0s (not to forget of course those beautiful single wheelers) with their decorative splashers very much like those to be found on the Midland, would undoubtedly have looked very well, an imagination easily borne out by the fact that some Glasgow & South Western engines of very similar appearance did indeed look very fine in their new LMS guise. On the other hand, one cannot quite visualise, say, the graceful Atlantics sitting very happily with the crimson lake, and many years later we were to witness the incongruous sight of a blue King on the GWR, a desecration fortunately short lived.

A further early anticipation of the Railways Act was the absorption of the Hull & Barnsley by the North Eastern on 1 April 1922.

Yet another proposal at the time was to form a separate group of all the railways roughly north of the Border—Carlisle and Newcastle would have been the obvious frontiers—which of course is what in the main happened twenty-five years later in the regional set-up at nationalisation. This would, however, have had obvious operating disadvantages, with the through traffic between England and Scotland. A mobile system such as a railway is surely best served by having its boundaries governed by its through routes rather than by box-like specified areas, a concept which was largely ignored in more recent times when the creation of regional boundaries has chopped mercilessly through some main lines, which in consequence lie through two or even three different operating areas. Full details of the composition of the new groups as eventually decided will be found in the appendix on page 27.

It will be interesting, however, at this stage to give brief descriptions of the four new railways which had come into being, particularly from the point of view of the motive power departments, and general changes in the locomotive scene which were to result.

The London Midland and Scottish Railway
(Route Mileage—excluding Irish Lines—7,790)

This was not only the largest of the four groups, it was actually the largest railway, with the possible exception of state systems, in the whole world.

For a full general history of the LMS one cannot do better than refer to a recent book on the subject by Hamilton Ellis, whilst the complete and intriguing story of its locomotives can be found in a finally definitive account by Mr E. S. Cox, who, holding an important key position in the CME's department, has been able to cover the subject completely from first-hand knowledge in his *Locomotive Panorama*—Volume One.

Very briefly, this may be summarised by recalling that Mr G. Hughes, formerly of the LY & R, became the first LMS chief mechanical engineer, from 1923 to 1925, when he was succeeded by Sir Henry Fowler, who had previously held this post for the last fifteen years of the Midland Railway's existence. Fowler remained in office until 1931, when he was replaced for a short time by Ernest Lemon, who, however, was not a locomotive man and did not produce any new engines. He was later to make his name in his real natural capacity in the operating and commercial spheres. It was the appointment of William (later Sir William) Stanier in 1932 which completely revolutionised locomotive development on the LMS, which had so far, with a few exceptions, perpetuated the small-engine policy inherited from the Midland under Sir Henry Fowler. Many engines of former MR design had been built during the early period, good enough designs within their capacity, particularly of course the famous Deeley compounds, but none of them adequate for the heaviest expresses. The class 4 goods, which continued to be built in large numbers to as late as 1940, totalled no less than 772 engines, exceeded only by Stanier's ubiquitous 'Black Fives', ultimately 842 in number.

One cannot mention the LMS, however briefly, without a reference to Sir Josiah Stamp, chairman from 1927 until his untimely death in an air raid in 1941, who laboured so hard and unremittingly in its cause during those years.

The London & North Eastern Railway
Route Mileage—6590

This was the second largest of the four groups; the backbone was of course the main line between London and Edinburgh, over the tracks of the former Great Northern, North Eastern, and North British Railways. The geographical situation of the Great Eastern, serving the whole of East Anglia, also brought it naturally into the LNER, but this was not so obvious in the case of the Great Central, which might have been allied with the Midland. The North Eastern, the largest of the constituents, had an almost complete monopoly of the counties of Durham and Northumberland, and largely so of Yorkshire. Further north, in addition to the North British, the LNER included the Great North of Scotland. There were also a few minor lines.

The rather obvious choice of chief mechanical engineer for the LNER was Nigel Gresley (he received his knighthood later), who was to earn lasting fame as the designer of the A4 Pacifics, and incidentally for his vigorous defence of steam propulsion as against diesel, which was in 1935 seriously considered in connection with the new high-speed services between London and Newcastle, and later Edinburgh. Sir Nigel fully justified his contention that he could do anything with steam that could be achieved by diesel, at that stage of its development. He was a broad-minded man, and continued for a few years to build not only his own designs, but some of the best of those of his former contemporaries, J. G. Robinson of the Great Central (a new series of Director 4-4-0s for Scotland and some A5 4-6-2Ts), and A. J. Hill of the Great Eastern (D16 super Clauds, B12 4-6-0s, and N7 0-6-2Ts) and most surprisingly. the 1898 design of Wilson Worsdell's J72 0-6-0Ts. (These were even perpetuated still further by BR in 1951, a situation without parallel elsewhere.)

The Great Western Railway
Route Mileage—3703

'Partner' is hardly the word which can be applied to any of the railways which constituted the make up of the new Great Western, as it could in the case of the other groups. In this case it was a matter of the absorption by one large company of a number of smaller ones, details of which can be found in the appendix (page 28).

The Great Western had always been a most individual line—it even contrived to remain so after nationalisation in 1948—and naturally its policies and ideas very soon eclipsed any characteristics possessed by the smaller lines which it took over. This was nowhere more noticeable than in the locomotive department, where for many years a Great Western engine had been so different from anything to be found elsewhere as to be recognisable on sight even by the less initiated, even if only by its characteristic Swindon boiler with its brass safety valve cover in the position where one normally expected to find a dome. This distinguishing feature had been introduced by William Dean at the turn of the century, and was to be perpetuated by his successors, G. J. Churchward (1902-21), C. B. Collett (1921-41), and F. W. Hawksworth (1941-8). Churchward came to a tragic end after his retirement by being run over by one of his own engines on 19 December 1933.

The GWR soon got to work on the very miscellaneous assortment of locomotives it acquired at the grouping, principally from the South Wales lines. Many were very soon scrapped and replaced by GWR standard types, quite a lot were rebuilt, some being scrapped not long afterwards, but a number of the best of them, notably from the Taff Vale and the Rhymney, survived into the nationalisation era.

The Southern Railway
Route Mileage—2200

The newly created company was not without its troubles in its early years. During 1924 and 1925 there were many complaints from the public of late running of trains and serious overcrowding. In defence the company displayed large full-page advertisements in the national newspapers stating their plans for the immediate future. A total of ninety-one new engines was to be built or purchased, and further electrification, already in progress on the South Western and Brighton sections, was to be extended to the South Eastern, and some of this was in operation by 1926.

Mr R. E. L. Maunsell, of the South Eastern, had been appointed chief mechanical engineer on the foundation of the SR, Mr R. W. Urie, of the LSWR, and Col L. B. Billinton, of the Brighton, having retired.

Mr Maunsell proceeded to build a fleet of modern and very efficient engines, mainly to his own designs, during the ensuing years, firstly by the purchase from the Government of fifty of his very successful N class 2-6-0s, which he had introduced on the SE & CR in 1917. The parts of these had been made at Woolwich after the end of 1921 to relieve unemployment, but had never been assembled. These did much to alleviate shortage of motive power, particularly in the west country. He also built a further twenty of the corresponding 2-6-4Ts (one with three cylinders), but these had a short and unhappy life. After several derailments there was a disastrous accident at Sevenoaks on 24 August 1927 when No A800 came off the road at high speed with much loss of life. All twenty-one engines were immediately taken out of service pending investigations, which subsequently showed that it was the poor state of the road rather than any defect in the design which was at fault, but nevertheless all were subsequently rebuilt as 2-6-0 tender engines. Some of the tank parts were later used to build further 2-6-4Ts for local freight work, but these were always strictly banned from working passenger trains. It is interesting to note that the LMS introduced the 2-6-4T type at about the time for fast suburban and semi-express work; several hundred of them were built and ran successfully right through to the end of steam.

Mr Maunsell's well-known King Arthur class of 1925 was an improved version of Urie's 1918 engines. In 1926 came the four-cylinder Lord Nelsons, principally for work on the heavy Continental trains on the South Eastern section, the engineering restrictions over which were gradually being removed by bridge strengthening to permit the much needed use of heavier engines.

To remember only one other design of Maunsell's, perhaps outstanding above all were the Schools class, introduced in 1930, a three-cylinder 4-4-0, regarded by many as the most successful design of this wheel arrangement ever built. There were forty of them in all, the last coming out in 1934, at which time there were also appearing the last batch of Gresley's Shire class on the LNER, and these were destined to be the last of that wheel arrangement to be built in Great Britain, although it was built for use in Ireland until as recently as 1948 (this does not include the GWR Dukedogs of 1936, which were no more than reconstructions). The last of the famous LMS compounds had been turned out in 1932, and it is an interesting sidelight to note that by pure coincidence both the Southern Schools and the final batch of LMS compounds were numbered 900-939, on their respective railways.

Mr Maunsell was succeeded in 1937 by the highly individual O. V. S. Bulleid, but as the first of his somewhat revolutionary designs did not appear until 1941 they do not come within the scope of the present book.

Joint Lines

There were over a hundred separate concerns at the time of the grouping, large and small, amongst which were a large number jointly owned or worked by two or more companies.

Where these were absorbed by one or other of the new railways, they fell naturally into the composition of the new company, but in a considerable number of cases the previous joint owners came into different groups, and inevitably these had to continue as joint railways, usually retaining their old titles, for another twenty-five years until nationalisation. The chief of these were the Midland & Great Northern Joint (LMS & LNER), Somerset & Dorset (LMS & SR), and the Cheshire Lines Committee (LMS & LNER). The first two of these were in effect still independent railways for the time being, even maintaining their individual locomotives and rolling stock, together with their own workshops for a number of years. The full story of all the jointly owned and operated lines may be found in the authors' book, *Britain's Joint Lines*.

The Metropolitan and Metropolitan District Railways

The inauguration of the London Passenger Transport Board in 1933 comprised the whole of the Underground tube system, the Metropolitan and the Metropolitan District Railways, together with the then still extensive tramway network and all public omnibuses, of which there were a number of small private operators apart from the main fleet owned by the London General Omnibus Company.

Of these, only the Metropolitan, and to a lesser extent, the Metropolitan District, concern us here. The Metropolitan celebrated its Diamond Jubilee on 10 January 1923. It was at that time promoting an intensive publicity campaign to attract not only visitors to the very attractive countryside which it served, the most unspoiled area within a radius of thirty miles of London, but also potential commuters. Its outward country end remained steam worked right through the period between the wars, and indeed until as late as 1960, the change-over from electric traction being made in earlier years at Harrow, and, in later years at Rickmansworth. For this purpose electric locomotives had to be provided to work the through trains into the inner London area to Liverpool Street or Aldgate.

Electric locomotives, as distinct from multiple unit trains, were very rare in this country until recent times. The Metropolitan District also had some, however, which worked in pairs between Ealing Broadway and Barking, a service of through trains which used to run between Ealing and Southend over the old London Tilbury & Southend system.

Independent and Light Railways

A number of small railways were in fact for some reason or another excluded from the provisions of the Railways Act of 1921. These are listed in the appendix, page 29. Some were narrow gauge, some standard gauge, many having been constructed under the Light Railways Act of 1896, designed to facilitate the construction and working of small lines by exempting them from certain requirements necessary in the case of main-line railways, such as signalling and continuous braking systems. An individual who did a good deal in the years immediately preceding World War I was one Lieutenant-Colonel H. F. Stephens, who seems to have been something of an early railway enthusiast, apart from his purely business interests in this field. He acted as manager, engineer, and in other capacities, a sort of 'Pooh Bah' in fact, to several concerns of this nature until his death on 23 October 1931. Chief among these were the Rother Valley Railway (later and still known as the Kent & East Sussex, which a preservation society is endeavouring to reopen), the Weston Clevedon & Portishead, the Shropshire & Montgomeryshire, a resuscitation of an older line, the Potteries Shrewsbury & North Wales, originally opened in 1866, twice closed and reopened, the Chichester & Selsey,* and the comparatively late East Kent, opened in 1911. For working these lines, he managed by shopping around to acquire the most fascinating collection of locomotives to be found anywhere, some of the industrial type, Manning Wardle and the like, but a fair number obtained cheaply from the main-line railways which had no further use for them, principally the LSWR, LB & SCR, and SE & CR.

*This line's official title at closure on 19 January 1935 was the West Sussex Railway. It had, however, been known at various times as the Chichester & Selsey Railway and Hundred of Manhood & Selsey Tramway (often abbreviated to just Selsey Tramway).

Irish Railways

At the end of World War I the whole of Ireland was still part of the United Kingdom. Following the 'troubles' of the ensuing years the Irish Free State, with the status of a British Dominion, officially came into being on 15 January 1922. This comprised the whole of the southern, western and north-western parts of the country, only the six counties in the north east, which constituted part of Ulster,* remaining part of the UK.

The railways, of which there were about some twenty different companies, retained their independence for the time being, but in 1925 all the systems lying wholly within the Free State were amalgamated into one, much on the lines of the English 1923 grouping. The new concern was known as the Great Southern. Railways which lay partly in the north and partly in the Free State, of which the Great Northern was the principal, and all those contained entirely in Northern Ireland, remained separate concerns until after World War II.

Outside the major cities of Dublin and Belfast, and a few smaller ones such as Cork, Waterford, and Londonderry, Ireland is quite a sparsely inhabited country, one of the few in the world with a declining population, and consequently its railways, away from the principal main lines, and around the few large centres of population, were mainly rural in character, often with two or three trains a day being found adequate or economic to run. Between the wars the country was a sheer delight to the enthusiast, each railway with its own individuality, and on most lines a large variety of elderly locomotives and coaching stock, contemporary with about thirty years earlier on this side of the Irish Sea, were to be found. This is not to say that services and upkeep were in any way decrepit, indeed on some railways, particularly the Great Northern, always a most enterprising company, they were very high, as they were on the Great Southern main line between Dublin and Cork, and on the Northern Counties Committee, formerly owned by the Midland Railway, and which had by then become part of the LMS system. There were two gauges in use, the main lines being 5ft 3in, on which the extra six inches was often found to give just that little extra degree of roominess and comfort compared with the English standard 4ft 8½in.

*The old Kingdom of Ulster consisted of nine counties, three of which were incorporated in the Free State.

The narrow gauge of 3ft was also widely used in the more remote parts, sometimes for quite lengthy lines; indeed, the main line of the Londonderry & Lough Swilly, with its Burtonport extension, through the wild north-west region of Donegal, was seventy-four and a half miles, with a journey time of roughly four hours, a fascinating experience. Nearly all of these lines, of which there were about a dozen, survived to World War II, but regrettably not one now remains. What is left of the Irish railway system, which in the Free State, later known as Eire, but now more often referred to as The Irish Republic, has not suffered from closures to anything like the same extent, proportionately, as in Britain, is now completely dieselised, and run in an exceedingly efficient and enterprising manner by the state-owned Coras Iompar Eireann, as it is now known.

The Railway Scene in General

AFTER SEVERAL years of hard wear and abnormally heavy traffic, coupled with inevitable depreciation of standards of maintenance, the railways emerged from the war in run-down condition and in poor shape for facing up to the difficulties with which they would have to contend in the ensuing years, strikes, trade depression, and above all, road competition.

At the beginning of the 1920s, railways were still the most important, and in many cases, the only means of communication for both passengers and freight. The menace of the internal combustion engine, although by no means a new invention, was still only a straw in the wind. It had already been experimented with in a small way on railways as a possible alternative to steam, but had not so far been seriously considered. It was in fact only just beginning to rear its head to any considerable extent on the roads, principally in the form of the omnibus, but even here only in urban areas and for short-distance country services. The lorry likewise was only in its infancy, while the private motor car was still something of a rarity.

Country roads were not macadamised to any extent; the solitary car still raised behind it an enveloping cloud of dust. As for the aeroplane, although it had developed sufficiently to take some part in World War I, it was not yet seriously considered as a practical means of passenger transport. If any competition was then thought of from this quarter, it was more in the direction of the airship, particularly the Zeppelin, which the Germans had by then developed to a considerable extent. In fact, but for the tragic disaster to the R101 on 5 October 1930, followed a few years later by the loss of the *Hindenburg* in New Jersey, USA, this form of air travel might well have developed alongside the heavier-than-air machine which we have today.

At the end of the war, many demobbed soldiers spent their gratuities on lorries or buses, setting up their own one-man businesses in opposition to the railways on a very small scale, and obviously only where traffic would be most lucrative. It did, however, sow the first seeds of competition which was to grow to alarming proportions in the years to come. Branch lines in particular were the first to feel the draught. Too often, the stations were situated too far from the centre of the towns or villages they served. Omnibuses were getting less unreliable in operation and able to travel longer distances at higher speeds, whilst the charabanc (or motor coach, as it later became) was also developing to the extent that it was beginning to encroach on some of the more lucrative holiday traffic. Nevertheless it seemed to take a long time before the railways woke up to the fact that their livelihood was being threatened, or for them to evolve any active measures to combat the danger.

Some steps were certainly taken, principally by the Great Western, to meet the competition, chiefly by the construction of a large number of unstaffed halts at points more convenient to the localities they served, but this was at best only a palliative and could not survive the ultimate greatest threat of all, the private motor car. That a large proportion of the population now possess its own private transport is a situation in a changing world to which from a railway point of view there is no answer and which has to be accepted. In pregrouping days some railways had run local bus services, but since World War I had no powers for operating their own motor transport. However, the Road Traffic Act of 1930, which embraced both passenger and goods traffic, did something towards controlling the chaotic and unfair position which had arisen. Another step taken was to obtain a part controlling interest in some of the competing omnibus companies, but not usually to the railways' real advantage.

So it was that the early 1930s saw the beginnings of branch line closures which, after the hiatus of World War II, was to proceed on an ever-increasing scale, culminating with the drastic slaughter of more recent years under the dead hand of Beeching. By this time the railways had indeed at last recognised the real threat to their monopoly, and launched a massive press campaign: 'Give the railways a square deal', which of course they never really got. The battle was too one-sided from the start. The railways' main contention was that whereas they had all the enormous overhead expense of providing and maintaining their own track and installations, their competitors had theirs provided free or practically free in the form of roads and signalling, either by traffic lights, then a comparative rarity, or more often by a policeman on point duty. It is true that these expenses were met to a small extent from the road fund licences and fuel tax, but these were very light compared with today's and the number of vehicles on the road was also very small in comparison. The question as to whether road users even today do really pay their share in upkeep of existing roads, let alone new construction, is at least open to argument, but would be inappropriate here.

Before leaving the subject of branch-line and cross-country services, mention should be made of the development of the railcar as a means of reducing the working costs of operating these lines, which even in the days before competition never, because of comparatively sparse population, really enjoyed very lucrative traffic.

In a final endeavour to reduce the expense of running such lines the combined single unit steam rail motor found favour on some railways in the opening years of the century, but had operational disadvantages, the chief of which was that they were not usually powerful enough to take an additional trailer in time of exceptional traffic. Nevertheless the Great Western had at one time no less than ninety-nine of them, some of which remained in active service until the 1930s. On other lines there were not very many left by 1920, but the Lancashire & Yorkshire, the second largest user, still retained its fleet of eighteen, two of which even survived the second war, the last of their kind.

The natural development of the combined engine and coach unit was the use of separate locomotives with one (or more) coaches, the end compartment adapted as a driving cab, with remote control, at first by means of pulleys and cables and later operated by vacuum or compressed air. A brake lever was of course provided in the driving compartment. This arrangement avoided the necessity of uncoupling and running round at the terminals. These rail motors, or pull-and-push trains lasted in some areas almost until the end of steam, but intermediately between their first introduction and the diesel railcar, referred to elsewhere, was the geared high-speed engine with a high working pressure developed by the Sentinel wagon works and Clayton Wagon Company. For rail passenger purposes these again, like the steam rail motors, took the form of a combined engine and coach body. The LNER had a large number of them, rather fascinatingly named after old-time stage coaches, and the LMS also had a few. Both railways, together with the Somerset & Dorset, also used the design adapted as a shunting engine. Unfortunately none of these interesting passenger vehicles, or any of the steam railcars, have survived to be preserved, although a Sentinel steam shunter can still be found on the Middleton Railway.

The period between 1929 and 1934 saw the great trade depression, which reached its peak in 1932. The misery of widespread unemployment was vividly portrayed in the film *Love on the Dole*, one of the classics in the history of the cinema. The effect on the railways was naturally widespread, heavy mineral traffic such as coal and iron ore being particularly affected, resulting in the temporary cancellation of orders for new engines and equipment, with many others laid off, a sight never seen before, although unfortunately a not uncommon one in more recent years.

Passenger traffic suffered too, apart from the substantial effects of road competition, and the value of shares fell sharply, the LNER coming off the worst in this respect, with the GWR and Southern the least affected.

By this time, the railways had at long last come

to realise that they no longer held a monopoly in transport, and had already begun to take really active steps to meet the competition. The Road Transport Act of 1928 had given the necessary powers to use motor road haulage, and some progress had been made towards co-ordination of rail and road transport in the form of goods collection and delivery, but it was not enough to stem the gradual diversion of traffic from railways to roads in general. The railways were reluctant to ask the Railway Rates Tribunal to give authority to raise fares and rates, as they realised that such a step would divert still more traffic and result even in a loss rather than a gain in revenue. In fact, by 1936, a very large proportion of passenger traffic—some 86 per cent—was being conveyed by some form of reduced fare facilities, cheap day returns, summer excursions, and other special tickets, and only 14 per cent at full standard fares. With regard to goods traffic, the railways were handicapped to some extent by the fact that they had to publish their rates, which road transport operators therefore knew, and could undercut.

Timings and Services

With the return of better times for the country as a whole, in the later 1930s (until for the second time within a generation everything had to give place to the fight for very existence and survival), there came the period regarded by many as the 'Golden Age of Railways'. This is not to belittle present-day exploits of Inter-City Expresses and the like, at speeds then undreamed of and which would have been quite impracticable under steam operation, but this must be viewed against the background of the general overall contraction of the railway system in general.

An innovation introduced by the LNER during 1928 was the fitting of some of the Gresley Pacifics with corridor tenders giving access between locomotive and train, with the object of carrying a spare crew who could change over in the course of the journey. This was to enable trains to run non-stop over the 392 miles between London and Edinburgh, a feat never before attempted. It was all put forward with much blare of publicity, but the LMS did not let the challenge go unanswered. Without any previous announcement, shortly before the new LNER service was due to start, they quietly divided the 10.00 am from Euston one morning into two portions, one for Glasgow and one for Edinburgh, the former hauled by a Royal Scot No 6113 *Cameronian* and the latter by 4-4-0 compound No 1054. All that had been done was to splay out the coal racks of the tenders to enable them to carry sufficient extra fuel for the trip. Without any ballyhoo the two engines completed their non-stop runs without difficulty. It was not repeated, and was really no more than a somewhat defiant gesture—'cocking a snoot', to use a more modern phrase—on the part of the LMS, as much as to say: 'We can do it if we want to!' But it did certainly steal some of the LNER's thunder.

The fastest train in the country at the time of the grouping was to be found on the North Eastern, whose 8.59 pm Darlington-York covered the forty-four miles in forty-three minutes, at that time the only train publicly booked start to stop at less than 'even time'. The Great Central newspaper express was booked in the July 1922 working timetable to cover the 22·6 miles from Leicester (dep 4.30 am) to Nottingham Arkwright Street in 22 minutes (arrive 4.52 am), but only the departure time, 4.57 am, showed in the public timetable. The Great Western advertised a timing of 105 minutes for the 106¼ miles from Paddington to Bath (61.1 mph) by the 11.15 am and 1.00 pm trains, but these were by means of slip coaches. All of these timings were matched by the Great Western on 9 July 1923, when it retimed its 2.30 pm from Cheltenham to Paddington, 77 miles, in 75 minutes. This record was eclipsed in 1928 with the same train, under the title of 'Cheltenham Flyer', when the time was cut to seventy minutes, an overall scheduled speed which had not before been seen in this country. This was but a prelude to what was to follow in the 1930s.

The appearance of Gresley's streamlined Pacific *Silver Link* in September 1935 caused much stir at the time, and a good deal of unfavourable comment from an aesthetic point of view, as nothing like it had been seen before. It certainly took some getting used to, but the success in operation of this famous class is too well known to need recapitulation here. The first four engines *Silver Link*, *Quicksilver*, *Silver King*, and *Silver Fox*, inaugurated the new high-speed service between Newcastle and London, 268½ miles in 240 minutes, the train being known as the 'Silver Jubilee', engine and coaches being painted in aluminium. Their later successors were employed on similar high-speed services, such as London to Edinburgh in six hours, whilst from an individual locomotive record point of view the exploit of *Mallard* on 3 July 1938, when it achieved a world-wide fully authenticated maximum speed with steam traction of 126 mph, has never since been surpassed. By 1939 there were more than a hundred regular daily

15

trains timed at an average speed of 60 mph or more.

The LMS also acquired a taste for streamlining in 1937 with a new series of Stanier Pacifics for working on a new high-speed train, the 'Coronation Scot' between Euston and Glasgow, now covered in six and a half hours. This was introduced on 5 July 1937, concurrently with a corresponding rival train on the LNER, the 'Coronation', King's Cross to Edinburgh in six hours. From a visual point of view the new LMS engines were even more startling, and to conservative eyes, ugly, than the LNER A4s. After two years we were beginning to get used to the wedge shaped outline of the latter which by then seemed rather preferable to the bulbous shape of the new LMS engines. Fortunately in this case the fashion did not persist indefinitely, as later examples were built to conventional design, and all of the others were eventually destreamlined before their final demise. One of them (still in streamlined form) No 6229 *Duchess of Hamilton* temporarily exchanged identities with the original No 6220 *Coronation* when it went to the USA in 1939 for the New York World Fair. It was still there on the outbreak of war and it was not found possible to bring it back until 1940. It was by no means the first time that a British engine had run on American railways, there being two other instances even within the period between the wars, the visit of *King George V*, GWR No 6000, to the Baltimore and Ohio centenary exhibition in 1927 and of LMS No 6100 *Royal Scot*, which toured both the USA and Canada in 1933.

On the subject of train services in general, to go back again to the beginning of the period under review, even to cover to a moderate extent the pattern of train facilities between the wars would require at least a large volume to itself, and within the present confines it is only possible to refer briefly to some of the more notable developments and achievements.

By the middle of 1919 some sort of start towards restoration of pre-war timings over the main lines was under way. Glasgow came once again within nine and a half hours of London by the West Coast route and ten and a half hours on the more difficult Midland line. Aberdeen was twelve and three-quarter hours from King's Cross and Inverness fifteen hours away from Euston. The Great Western held pride of place with the longest non-stop run in the country between Paddington and Plymouth, 225¾ miles in 262 minutes by the Cornish Riviera. The South Eastern had already actually improved on its best pre-war timing between London and Margate, now 90 minutes for 74 miles by the best trains, most creditable in view of the difficult and congested nature of the road. The Great Central, that enterprising company always to the fore, also smartened up its services in competition with its chief rival, the Midland, with such short snippets as a timing of twenty-one minutes for the nineteen and a half miles between Rugby and Leicester, admittedly a lightly loaded night-time newspaper train, but nevertheless indication of its general progressive spirit.

The year 1922 saw the introduction of the most intensive steam-operated suburban service ever seen either in Great Britain or anywhere else in the world, over the Great Eastern network out of Liverpool Street. Under the vigorous leadership of Sir Henry Thornton, the general manager, it was decided as an alternative to the expense of electrification, already much in the air, to increase the line capacity to its fullest extent, to see what could be done with continued steam working, a project which was fulfilled to a remarkable extent by F. V. Russell, appointed superintendent of operation for the purpose. Amongst the many measures taken was the provision at Liverpool Street of a separate engine bay for each platform, from which, with ultra-smart operation the waiting engine would already be following an incoming train into the platform before this had even come to a halt. The train could be then ready to depart in no more time than it took to uncouple the locomotive of the arriving train, disgorge the passengers, and take on a fresh load—away again in as little as a couple of minutes, shorter than the time taken by the motormen of electric multiple units at Waterloo to lock up the front driving cab and to proceed to the outer end of the train. So much for the much-vaunted time-saving convenience of multiple unit operation. This of course was only one detail of the vast operation, which included such considerations as carefully worked-out timings to the half minute to avoid conflicting train movements at intersections. At the business peak periods it was found possible to run trains over the same tracks with a headway of only two and a half minutes, twenty-four trains an hour, each with a seating capacity of 848 (and which with standing passengers often carried over 1000 per train). And when it is remembered that this intensive service was worked by small and ageing 0-6-0T, 2-4-2T, and 0-4-4Ts—the larger N7 0-6-2Ts had only just started to appear—this stands out as one of the most remarkable feats of local steam working ever seen. This was known as the 'Jazz' service, consequent on the practice then newly adopted of painting, for quick identification, a yellow stripe over the doors of the first-class compartments, nowadays of course a practice universally adopted by BR, together with a blue stripe over the second, at that time an intermediate class between first and the then third class. The word 'jazz' had just reached this country from America, associated not only with dance music, but with brightness and colour. To maintain such exacting requirements a high standard of maintenance was of course essential. Failures were rare, and the deplorable standards of upkeep which were to become so regrettably common in later years were at that time unknown. As a result, it was fourteen years before thoughts were again turned towards electrification, and then, owing to the incidence of World War II, yet another fourteen years were to elapse before it became an established fact. The soulless efficiency of electrification was of course bound to win in the end, but nowhere else would such a fine rearguard action against heavy odds be found as in the last days of Great Eastern steam.

So far as the general convenience of train services between the wars and comparison with those appertaining today is concerned (apart from actual line closures) the point that strikes one is the present day standardised type of service, stopping only at principal stations, with connecting services —too often only in uncomfortable multiple diesel units—to subsidiary towns and branches, where there are any left at all. Through carriages to destinations off the principal routes are now all too much of a rarity. One has only to recall, for instance, the lovely train the Atlantic Coast Express, which left Waterloo every weekday, a train of perhaps a dozen or so vehicles embracing through coaches to such places as Seaton, Exmouth, Ilfracombe, Bude, and all detached at the appropriate junction and worked forward by the branch engine, with the remaining rump of the train, including restaurant car, perhaps ending up at Padstow (the actual pattern changed over the years).

Then there was that ubiquitous through train between Aberdeen and Penzance, introduced on 3 October 1921, with its coach headboards appropriately labelled 'Aberdeen & Penzance via Edinburgh, York, Sheffield, Leicester, Swindon & Plymouth' and running over the metals of four railways, the North British, North Eastern, Great Central, and Great Western. The word 'train' was perhaps something of a misnomer, as normally only one brake composite coach worked throughout, with the addition of an extra third in the summer. These were provided alternately by the North British and Great Western Railways. The train consisted only of the through coaches—plus restaurant car—between Westbury and York, in the northern direction, and between York and Swindon, southbound. Restaurant facilities were provided throughout, and first-class sleeping car or cars were attached between York and Aberdeen on the northbound journey and Swindon and Penzance in the other direction. Outside these limits there would be parts of through trains serving other destinations. The through journey of 785 miles, the longest in the British Isles, occupied some twenty-four hours. Whilst it was hardly to be expected that there would be more than a few through passengers between the two extremities, and it could hardly have been designed with this object in view, it did nevertheless provide a most useful through means of communication between the many important towns served en route. In a small way, this train might perhaps be regarded as a miniature counterpart of the famous cosmopolitan trans-Europe expresses of former days, so beloved of the romantic fiction writers of the time, on which, so one reads, there would be the inevitable beautiful and seductive female spy. However, the chances of becoming involved in a similar encounter, with its subsequent story of espionage and intrigue, one would imagine to be extremely remote on a journey, say, between Banbury and Rotherham!

There were many other such through facilities, which in the period between the wars reached their maximum, but few of which survive today, except in very truncated form. Notable were the through expresses, mainly of a limited holiday seasonal character, between the Midlands and the south coast resorts, which avoided the inconvenience of a transfer between London terminal stations. These chiefly concerned the London & North Western, London Brighton & South Coast, and South Eastern & Chatham Railways, in providing through services, mainly at weekends during the summer period, between Liverpool, Manchester, Birmingham, and similar places, and Brighton, Eastbourne, Margate, and the various south coast resorts. These ran via Willesden Junction, where LMS engines were exchanged for SR, and the West London line via Clapham Junction or Longhedge Junction, according to destination. The Brighton one held the distinction of being an actual named train, the Sunny South Express. There were also comparable trains from the LNER via the GCR, Oxford, Reading and Redhill.

Away from London, there were the similar trains between the north country and the east coast over the Midland & Great Northern Joint Railway, now unfortunately no more, such remnants of the services as still survive having been directed over the lines of the former Great Eastern.

Through communication between the Midland and the South Western were provided over the route of the Somerset & Dorset Joint Railway, another regrettable casualty, the principal train being eventually well known as the Pines Express, which in 1939 was running daily between Manchester and Liverpool and Bournemouth, via Birmingham, Bath and the S & DJR.

The principal resorts in the west country, such as Torquay, Paignton, and Newquay, were well served during the summer season with through trains between these areas and the midlands and north east, Sheffield, Leeds, Bradford, and so on, some of which survive even today; to a greater extent in fact than most of the others already mentioned.

Even in prewar days cross-country journeys involving changes of trains could be an awkward and frustrating experience, now with the disappearance of so many connecting links such as the Oxford—Bletchley—Cambridge route, vitally important to the general network, even if on paper non-productive, it has become virtually impracticable in many areas.

An important innovation towards the end of 1936 was the inauguration jointly between the Southern Railway and the Nord Railway of France of through trains between London and Paris. The sleeping cars provided by the Continental Wagons-Lits were shunted on to the newly built ships *Shepperton Ferry* and *Hampton Ferry* operating between Dover and Dunkirk, and for the first time in history passengers could now enjoy an uninterrupted night's travel between the two capitals. The inaugural run for distinguished personalities such as Sir John Simon (Home Secretary), the general managers of the two railways, the British and French Ambassadors, etc, took place by a departure from Paris on 13 October 1936. On the British side the train was divided into two portions, each consisting of five Wagons-Lits, the first hauled by engines 939 and 1756, double headed, and the second by Lord Nelson, No 855, *Robert Blake*.

The first regular train from Victoria left at 10.00 pm on 14 October 1936, consisting of three ordinary coaches and a Pullman car (for passengers to destinations in Europe other than Paris) and six Wagons-Lits, plus two vans, and it was double headed by 4-4-0s Nos 1758 and 1470. Nelson No 854 *Howard of Effingham* took it on the second night, but the regular practice became to employ a couple of 4-4-0s of classes L or L1, sometimes relieved by a D1 or E1 rebuild. Naturally this useful and popular service had to be withdrawn at the outbreak of war.

Another facility of former years and particularly in pregrouping days, was provided by some lines, one of which was the Midland, in making conditional out-of-the-way stops at comparatively minor stations, on due notice being given, by some main-line trains, even London expresses. This practice does in fact still survive to a small extent on some railways such as the former Highland, in which connection I must recall a slightly embarrassing occasion I experienced in 1928, from which one wonders whether such facilities were much used even at that time. Returning from Wick to Inverness I needed to alight at Muir of Ord, as this happened to be the best way of 'doing' the Fortrose branch, which had to be fitted in somehow. The restaurant car was full of voluble Scotsmen when the guard came through the train: 'Everybody for Inverness?', whereon I piped up: 'I want to get out at Muir of Ord'. There was a sudden hushed silence, and one by one faces peeped round the central aisle to see what strange foreigner (as an unmistakable Southerner was regarded by the Scots) it could be who did not wish to go through to the capital city of the Highlands. Even the guard seemed momentarily disconcerted, but he quickly came back with: 'Och, mon, I'll have the train stopped for ye'. When I did alight, I was acutely conscious of fifty pairs of incredulous eyes watching my progress to the branch train already quietly simmering in the bay platform, a then frequent sight now, alas, gone for ever. The gladsome sight of the lovely Skye bogie with its two ancient six wheelers, however, quickly dispelled all other thoughts (illustration page 87).

Technical Innovation

A number of experimental locomotives were tried out on the main line railways during the period under review, embodying various forms of turbine, condensing, and high-pressure steam, but all with one possible exception destined in the light of later history, to be regarded either as failures or at the very least not having come up to expectations. Amongst them may be mentioned the Ljungstrom turbine locomotive of Swedish design, built by Messrs Beyer Peacock & Co in 1926 and which worked on the Midland section of the LMS for a considerable time. Several other experiments with turbine propulsion were also made during the period, but the only one which met with any marked success—after the inevitable teething troubles—was Stanier's LMS Pacific No 6202, built in 1935. This was a lovely engine to see in action, particularly its almost noiseless ascent up the one-in-seventy Camden bank on the 8.30 a.m. to Liverpool, its regular job for several years, which it handled with ease. One noticeable characteristic, not often referred to, was that in marked contrast to its sisters, it very rarely slipped on starting, possibly due to the more even torque compared with normal cylinder propulsion. In spite of its undoubted success, however, it showed no real advantage over the orthodox design, to which it was eventually converted in 1952 as *Princess Anne*, with a tragically short life, as it was damaged beyond repair in the disastrous Harrow accident.

Two important experiments in high-pressure steam must also be mentioned. The Royal Scot variant No 6399 *Fury*, was built as a compound with one high-pressure and two low-pressure cylinders supplied at no less than 900 lb per square inch. Unfortunately it ran into trouble after only a few trials, a burst water-tube killing an inspector on the footplate and it was ultimately rebuilt by Stanier with his design of orthodox taper boiler.

There was also Gresley's 'hush hush' engine built at Darlington in 1929 under conditions of great secrecy. When it emerged it turned out to be a semi-streamlined 4-6-4 (the largest passenger engine ever to run in these islands) four-cylinder compound No 10000, with 450 lb pressure Yarrow marine water-tube boiler, suitably adapted for a locomotive. This engine worked for several years with considerable success, but in 1937 was rebuilt with an ordinary boiler and thereafter much resembled the A4 Pacifics, although it still remained the only 4-6-4 in the country.

The general conclusion of all these and other experiments was that there was little or nothing to be gained by departing from the modernised but nevertheless conventional design of steam locomotive dating back over a century, and which in its general concept was to last until the very end of steam.

In 1938 the LMS and LNER jointly prepared plans for a locomotive testing station to be built at Rugby, but although construction was commenced the war halted its progress and it was not brought into use until 1948. The GWR had for many years had a small testing plant in its works at Swindon, on which the locomotives were mounted on 'wheels' instead of rails and could simulate high-speed running conditions whilst actually remaining stationary, 'running on the spot' in more modern phraseology.

An earlier event in the first days of the grouping had been the locomotive exchanges of 1925 and 1926. The 1925 trials were between the LNER and the GWR, between King's Cross and Doncaster and between Paddington and Plymouth. On the LNER the famous *Flying Scotsman* No 4472, then only two years old, was matched against No 4079 *Pendennis Castle*, an even newer engine, both of classes which were to achieve world-wide fame in later years. Although a smaller engine (the Kings had not yet seen the light of day) the GWR 4-6-0 was theoretically more powerful than its Pacific rival. Over the Great Western main line between Paddington and Plymouth the corresponding engines were LNER 4474 *Victor Wild* and GWR 4074 *Caldicot Castle*.

In 1926 there were further trials of a Castle, this time No 5000 *Launceston Castle*, which displayed its ability to deal with a 400 ton load between Euston and Carlisle, which it did with flying colours. These tests lasted five weeks. The LMS had at that time no large express engines of comparable dimensions or capabilities to effect a fair comparison, but they did send one of the Deeley compound 4-4-0s No 1047, the further construction of which was proceeding apace, over to the GWR where it worked between Paddington and Plymouth, but with essentially much lighter loads of 210 tons or so for which these engines were ideally suited.

For the full account of these trials and their assessment and effect on later locomotive development the reader must be referred elsewhere, in particular to a book by Mr Cecil J. Allen on the subject, *Locomotive Exchanges*, which includes other similar events which have taken place in the course of locomotive history.

Another exciting special event of a very different nature took place in July 1925 in the form of a three-day celebration held at Darlington by the LNER in tribute to the centenary of the opening of the Stockton & Darlington Railway in 1825. The highlight of the proceedings was an enormous procession of historic locomotives and rolling stock over part of the original route of the S & DR, made possible by the fact that much of it was no longer in use for ordinary passenger trains, and goods traffic could be suspended for a few hours.

The cavalcade proceeded steadily at intervals, fifty-three locomotives, trains, set pieces, and so on, past the grandstand which had been erected for the use of the VIPs including the Duke and Duchess of York (later King George VI and Queen Elizabeth), to view the proceedings, the ordinary public being able make use of a public road adjoining the line and adjacent fields to which the owners allowed access. The fine weather helped in no small way towards the enjoyment of this wonderful spectacle, the like of which had never been seen before and is unlikely to be seen again.

The corresponding centenary of the LMS took place five years later, in 1930, commemorating the opening of the Liverpool & Manchester Railway on 15 September 1830. This was not quite comparable with the goings-on at Darlington, consisting chiefly of a static exhibition of a handful of engines at Wavertree Park, Liverpool. They did, however, have the old Liverpool & Manchester engine *Lion* in steam on a circular track with a train of period replica coaches in which the public could ride. The old engine had been recently discovered on stationary boiler work at one of the Liverpool Docks, virtually unknown and forgotten but most fortunately found in time to ensure its preservation and restoration.

The Railway Network

The railway map of the British Isles was virtually complete by the turn of the century. The Great Central's extension to London was the last main line to be constructed (and has recently gained the unenviable distinction of being the first to be closed). A certain number of branch lines and light railways were built prior to the 1914 war but during the period under review new construction practically ground to a halt, since when, apart from new urban construction, such as the London Underground system and sundry connecting loops or diversions, practically nothing has been added but a very great deal has been lost and continues to be at a decreasing, but still disturbing pace.

The last standard-gauge really rural branch line to be built was the North Devon & Cornwall Junction Light Railway, Halwill Junction—Torrington, twenty and a half miles, opened on 27 July 1925, worked by the Southern Railway and in effect an extension of the LSWR system in the west country. (The first sod had actually been cut in 1921 by the Parliamentary Secretary to the newly formed Ministry of Transport.) The engineer was Lieutenant-Colonel Stephens, referred to in the section (page 12) devoted to light railways. This was a

country branch in the true sense, steam-worked right to its closure for through passenger working in 1965. The short Allhallows branch, opened for passenger traffic on 14 May 1932 (already in operation for goods since 1 March), might also be considered in the same category, although hardly rural in character. There were also two short extensions to the East Kent Light Railway, opened in 1925, one of which was a projected line through to Canterbury, which was never completed. The Wimbledon and Sutton line of the SR, opened in two sections on 7 July 1929 and 5 January 1930 respectively, was also comparatively new, as was the extension from Motspur Park to Chessington (29 May 1938 and 28 May 1939), both of these being additions to the SR suburban network, and of course worked electrically from the start. The Wimbledon & Sutton line had originally been intended to be worked by the Metropolitan District Railway, but the powers were transferred to the SR in 1924.

Amongst other new lines opened between the wars may be mentioned the Totton Hythe & Fawley, 20 July 1925, to serve the new oil refinery on Southampton Water. The Croxley Green & Watford line, built jointly by the Metropolitan and LNER, was opened on 2 November 1925, at first operated by trains of both companies, the LNER being steam worked and the Metropolitan electrically. This arrangement did not last long, and for many years it has been just a part of the Transport Board Network. The Metropolitan, on its own in this case, also constructed another new branch from Wembley Park to Stanmore, opened on 10 December 1932. This was built to full main-line Metropolitan loading gauge and was at first operated by its multiple unit electric trains. Later, however, these were replaced by through Bakerloo line trains from the Elephant & Castle, these being of course tube stock, since when the branch has been in effect an extension of the Underground system.

The British Empire Exhibition held at Wembley in 1924 and 1925 was the principal reason for the construction of a new loop line, single, and with running in only one direction, between the Aylesbury and High Wycombe lines at Neasden, over which a frequent service of trains could be operated without reversal at the newly built exhibition station, which had actually been used for the first time for the Cup Final at the adjoining Stadium on 28 April 1923. It was much utilised during subsequent years for the operation of trains in connection with football matches and other events held there. It was last used on 18 May 1968 and the line closed permanently on 1 September 1969. At the 1924/5 Exhibition the railways themselves had a large display stand, where were to be seen amongst other engines, *Flying Scotsman* and K3 2-6-0 No 200 from the LNER, GWR *Pendennis Castle*, LMS Horwich built 4-6-4T No 11114, and SR Maunsell 2-6-0 No A866.

In 1925 the GWR opened a new line in the area west of Wolverhampton, on which construction had begun in 1913, but had to be suspended owing to the war. It ran from Oxley Junction on the Shrewsbury main line southwards through pleasant countryside to join up with a much older line at Baggeridge Junction, which connected with the Stourbridge and Worcester line at Kingswinford Junction. Goods traffic commenced initially on a 'run if required' basis on 1 January 1925, and through passenger trains from Wolverhampton to Stourbridge via the new route on 11 May 1925. They were, however, shortlived, and ceased in 1932. As a through route the line was closed entirely in 1964.

Opened in sections during 1931/2 was a new line, seven and a half miles long, including some colliery branches, built jointly by the LMS and LNER between Farnsfield and New Ollerton, under the title Mid Nottinghamshire Joint Line. It was built principally for coal traffic and never had a passenger service.

The Ashover Light Railway was the last narrow-gauge railway (apart from pleasure lines and the like) to be opened in Great Britain. With a gauge of two feet, and a length of seven and a half miles, it was made to connect Ashover, a small and pleasant country town near Chesterfield, with the LMS main line at Clay Cross. Unfortunately it came too late for a railway of this sort; road transport was already well enough established to be able to cope with traffic of this nature. It had actually been authorised by the Ministry of Transport in 1919, but owing to delays in construction it was not opened until 6 April 1925. Passenger services lasted only for eleven years, and it closed altogether in 1950. There was also the Welsh Highland Railway in North Wales. The southern end of this was completed and opened in 1923, passenger services being operated until September 1936 and the line closed altogether in 1937. Mention should also be made of the Romney Hythe & Dymchurch Railway, which, although a miniature line with a gauge of only fifteen inches, was nevertheless more than a mere pleasure railway, such as are to be found at many seaside and other holiday resorts. It was opened in 1927 from New Romney to Hythe, a

distance of eight and a quarter miles, and extended to Dungeness, another five and a half miles, in 1928/9. As such it did, and still does, perform a useful service to the local inhabitants, apart from the numerous visitors who enjoy it for its own value.

Hardly coming within the category of new lines, in that they were not built to serve new towns or areas, were a number of new diversions, loops, and cutoffs. Amongst the most important of these were the new lines around Ramsgate, opened in 1926, when the SR decided to close the old LC & DR terminus at Ramsgate Harbour. Whether this was a wise decision in the light of later experience is questionable as the old station was quite literally on the sea front, which was where most visitors wished to go, particularly day trippers, with whom there was a lucrative traffic in the summer season. Admittedly it was cramped in accommodation, with an approach through a steeply graded tunnel at one in seventy-five, and awkward to operate, but it would not have been unduly so under present conditions with electric traction. Anyway, the new loop which was constructed to join up with the former SER line at Ramsgate Town was a considerable distance from the sea, and one cannot but wonder how much traffic was lost in consequence to the then growing army of road coach operators who could take their passengers straight through to the sea front. Another example of where the railways failed to appreciate and take steps to meet the growing threat of road competition. An amusement park was built on the site of the old railway station, and the tunnel bricked up, but ten years later the southern end was reopened with a two-foot gauge electric railway constructed by a private company to a point only a short distance from Dumpton Park station (which had been opened on 19 July 1926 to replace Ramsgate Harbour). A new length of narrow-gauge tunnel had to be bored at the top end. This useful connection operated, except during the war period from 1939 until 1945, during the summer months until 1965.

In Northern Ireland, the LMS carried out an enterprising scheme on its Northern Counties line by the construction of a large avoiding loop to obviate the reversal at Greenisland of all trains between Belfast and Portrush or Londonderry, which enabled expresses to be speeded up by as much as twenty minutes. It involved the construction of a large viaduct and was the only major new line to be constructed in Ireland between the wars. It was opened on 17 January 1934. Mention might, however, be made of the new double-decked

Craigavon road bridge at Londonderry, opened in 1933. This ancient city was served by four railway systems, two broad gauge and two narrow gauge, one of each set on either side of the river, and all without physical interconnection. These were the LMS-owned NCC main line from Belfast, the narrow-gauge line to Strabane (worked by the County Donegal) the GNR, and the Lough Swilly. The lower deck of the new bridge was laid out with mixed gauge for transfer of wagons between all four systems, worked by capstan and so far as is known never traversed by locomotives.

The Great Western, always on the ball when it came to a question of speeding up, decided to assist the acceleration of their West of England expresses by avoiding the awkward situations which existed at Westbury and Frome, both with severe speed restrictions. This was done by the construction of avoiding loops by-passing these points, and these were opened on 2 January 1933.

In the London area, the Southern Railway decided to utilise part of the abandoned Greenwich Park branch, which had been closed since 1917 (one of the very earliest branch line casualties in the Metropolis), to divert some of the through freight services between Hither Green and Hornsey which ran via London Bridge over the former LC & DR line via Nunhead and Blackfriars. For this purpose a new loop and viaduct was built at Lewisham and put into operation on 7 July 1930. From 30 September 1935 some passenger trains were also diverted by this route from Charing Cross to Holborn Viaduct to relieve congestion in the peak period.

Apart from sundry extensions to the London Underground system, these were about the only additions of any note to the railway map. There were a number of other projects, some actually authorised by the Ministry of Transport, amongst which may be mentioned a proposed light railway from Longridge to Hellifield. The most important and ambitious proposals (which never got as far as the authorisation stage) were made in 1920 for the development of the Highlands of Scotland. These included 226 miles of standard gauge to such outposts as Ullapool and Lochinver, in areas never touched by railways, and which now never will be, and 156 miles of narrow gauge on the Isle of Skye, Lewis, and Arran, again fascinating suggestions of what might have been. What lovely railways they would undoubtedly have become can now only be visualised in a world of make believe. Had they ever been built, they would have considerably changed the railway map of Scotland.

As it was, the only light narrow-gauge railway which that country ever enjoyed was the remote Campbeltown & Machrihanish, which managed to survive until 1931.

Electrification and Diesel Traction

Turning now to electrification, it was of course the Southern Railway which went in for this type of traction to a far greater extent than any other between the wars. Outside London and the southern counties electrification was only to be found in a few areas. Liverpool had the Mersey Railway and the Liverpool Overhead, the only elevated railway of its kind in the country, and now regrettably no more. The North Eastern had had some local electric services around Newcastle even since 1904, and on the Lancashire & Yorkshire the Liverpool-Southport and Manchester—Bury lines had also been electrified. This company had also experimented on its Holcombe Brook branch with 3,500 volt direct current supplied through overhead wires, all the other lines mentioned being on the third-rail system.

The Midland also had an experimental line in operation from Lancaster to Heysham, this again being with overhead current collection, 6,600 volt alternating current, similar to that which had been adopted by the LB & SCR. Around London the Metropolitan District was entirely electrically worked, as was the Metropolitan country 'main line' as far as Harrow, (later extended to Rickmansworth) beyond which steam remained in use until comparatively recently.

The LNWR had also electrified its local service between Euston and Watford, and the old North London from Broad Street to Richmond. Mention might also be made of the Swansea & Mumbles Railway in South Wales, incidentally the oldest passenger railway in the world, dating from 1807. It went through three phases, horse, steam, and, in 1929, electric, although in this case it became virtually a roadside tramway system.

Gradual extension of electrification over the Southern suburban system and later also on the Brighton, Eastbourne, and Portsmouth main lines, which took place between the wars, largely owing to the influence of Sir Herbert Walker, the general manager, vastly increased the frequency of the services and also reduced the timings, although this was not so marked on the longer runs. In the case of Brighton, in fact, the non-stop timing for the fifty and three-quarter miles remained at sixty minutes, which it had been for years in steam days. All this was at the cost of a serious deterioration in the standards of comfort. The earlier suburban units were appalling, and even the later main-line stock was not much better in this respect: the rough riding of the Brighton Belle Pullman sets became notorious. The noise from the electric pick-up shoes was also very bad, and the experienced rail traveller would always try to get a seat as far away from the power bogie as possible! A lot of the earlier suburban trains were very shoddy, many of them being conversions from old steam stock, and the heating was so poor as to be practically useless in very cold weather. The whole operation, in the earlier years at any rate, gave the impression of having been done 'on the cheap' with as little capital expenditure as possible.

Not only this, but the hard wear and tear which the trains had to undergo was not helped by the driving methods of some of the motormen, as they were now called, and their handling of the Westinghouse brake, with its much fiercer application than the vacuum brake to which they had been accustomed. Some of them never seemed to get used to using it in a sympathetic manner, their method being to run into a station at a full thirty miles per hour or so and to apply a full and vigorous application of the brakes at the last moment. Sometimes one was almost thrown to the floor in a train, hardly the acme of comfort expected in rail travel. (The image of 'Southern Electric' which the publicity department strove so hard to encourage was often irreverently called by regular travellers the 'Southern Epileptic'—but this is by the way.) The introduction of intensive electric traction also had its effect on the civil engineering side; the unsprung weight of the motor bogies was very hard on the track, and the costs of maintenance went up enormously. However, in spite of all its shortcomings, the operation was an undoubted overall success, so much so that the great increase in traffic became an embarrassment so far as the handling of the commuter services were concerned, particularly on the South Eastern section, a situation which persists today. A senior SR official, in the course of a lecture on electrification about 1930 did at least make a quiet dig at his own company by remarking that even if the SR was the smallest of the four railways it could at least claim the title of 'Britain's Premier Tramway'!

The Southern had inherited two entirely different systems of electrification at the grouping, the 6,600 volt alternating current with overhead wires which had been adopted by the LB & SCR and which dated back to 1909, and the 600 volt direct current third-rail system which the LSWR had

preferred when it introduced its first electric services in 1915. These two widely differing systems were by their very nature hardly compatible for simultaneous operation over the same tracks and were confined to their respective railways for the first few years of the grouping with extensions on both railways. The third-rail system was employed when a start was made on electrifying the SE & CR lines, hitherto entirely steam worked, in 1925. It was then becoming obvious that one system or the other would eventually have to be adopted as standard for the whole SR network, and in 1926 the decision was made in favour of the third rail. This was no doubt influenced by the fact that not only was it cheaper and quicker to install, but there was already very much more of it than of the LB & SCR overhead. As a long-term issue it is, however, very much open to doubt whether the decision was a wise one, as although third-rail current collection is more or less satisfactory for purely suburban working there are a number of reasons why it is not so for main-line operation, and had the SR had this eventual possibility more firmly in view it would have undoubtedly have been better advised to take the plunge and develop the overhead system. However, there it was, and the last LB & SCR overhead electric train ran in 1929, only four years after the final extension to Coulsdon had been made, incidentally with trains worked by separate electric locomotives sandwiched between two pairs of coaches. We now have the situation whereby whatever future electrification extensions there may be made on the other main-line railways there can never be a complete link up with the Southern system, which must inevitably remain a separate entity. Any question of conversion would be quite ruled out by the enormous cost that would be involved.

In 1930 the Ministry of Transport decreed that any future main-line electrification should be on the 1,500 volt direct current overhead system, and by way of preliminary trials the Manchester South Junction & Altrincham Railway, jointly owned by the LMS and LNER, was so converted.

In 1938 the old Wirral Railway of the LMS was electrified, joining up with the Mersey (then still independent), to which with through working it became a virtual extension. There was nothing in Scotland, unless one includes the Glasgow Subway underground line, converted in 1935 from cable operation, the last example of this form of haulage on a passenger railway in Great Britain, apart from the Great Orme Railway, Llandudno, still extant.

The only railway which in pregrouping years

had considered main-line electrification seriously was the North Eastern, which contemplated conversion of the main line between York and Newcastle. As an experiment the eighteen-and-a-half-mile stretch of mineral line between Shildon and Newport was equipped with 1,500 volt direct current, with overhead wires, and was partly worked by ten electric locomotives for a number of years, although this eventually fell into disuse with a complete reversion to steam haulage. A large electric locomotive was actually built in anticipation of the projected main-line passenger services, but it never had a chance to demonstrate its powers. It is worth noting that apart from the Manchester South Junction & Altrincham the LMS, LNER and GWR produced no new electrification between 1916 (Broad Street—Richmond) to 1930 (Wirral).

Although electrification in Ireland was practically non-existent, that country had, curiously enough, the distinction of having had the first electrically operated railway in the British Isles, the Giant's Causeway Tramway in Antrim, a three-foot gauge line opened on 29 January 1883 with steam working (tram engines of the enclosed type), electric operation being introduced on 18 September of the same year. As might be expected with such an innovation, various difficulties were encountered in the early stages, and steam had to be resorted to on many occasions during these earlier years. The line was some four and a half miles in length. It continued in operation until 1951.

The Volks' Electric Tramway, running along the seashore at Brighton, at first only a quarter of a mile in length, was essentially of an experimental nature, and being of such short length, more on the lines of the modern pleasure railway, and hardly came into the same category as the Giant's Causeway Railway. Nevertheless, this little system opened on 3 August 1883, actually preceding by a few weeks the commencement of electric working on the Giant's Causeway Railway, and should perhaps share the distinction of being Britain's first electric railway. Incidentally it is still in operation.

Another short line in Ireland was the Bessbrook & Newry, but apart from purely urban tramways in the cities of Dublin, Cork, and Belfast, these were the only electrified lines to be found in that country.

Mention should, however, be made of the introduction, as an alternative to full electrification of the old Dublin & South Eastern suburban lines, which was under consideration, of two twin articulated coach units powered by batteries. The constant need for recharging was something of an operating nuisance, but nevertheless the cars continued in use until after World War II.

The gradual development of the internal combustion engine for railway purposes really began between the wars, although the earliest experiments with petrol-driven railway vehicles took place in the middle 1900s, before World War I, in the form of single small passenger units or 'railcars', as they later became known. It was not until the earlier part of the period of the present review that the development of the oil engine, or 'diesel', began to appear, initially in the form of a converted L & YR four-coach electric set experimentally converted to diesel traction at Horwich in 1928. This was the first diesel multiple unit of the type with which we are familiar today, as distinct from a railcar (diesel or otherwise) which consists of a single vehicle.

The first of these appeared in 1931 on the three-foot gauge system on the County Donegal Railway in Ireland, and was followed in this country by a fleet of streamlined railcars on the Great Western, which appeared initially in 1933. The first diesel shunting locomotive seems to have been one constructed by Kerr Stuart in 1929 for the Ravenglass & Eskdale Railway, most of it a fifteen-inch gauge miniature railway, but which at that time had some two and a half miles of standard gauge serving a stone quarry. It was the LMS, however, which was the first main-line company to experiment with a diesel locomotive, in 1931. It was constructed on the frames of a Johnson 0-6-0T No 1831, which number the new creation inherited. Like the Eskdale locomotive, it had mechanical transmission, but was followed in 1933 by the introduction of the diesel-electric version, which formed the basis of a standard type since used in large numbers on British Railways.

The GWR and Southern introduced their own very similar versions in 1937, the Great Western having already experimented with a small diesel-mechanical locomotive, not very widely known, in 1933. (This company had also built five small four wheeled petrol shunting locomotives during the 1920s.)

Apart from the initial LMS experiment of 1928, no more diesel multiple units appeared again until 1938, when the LMS tried out a new three-car set on the Oxford—Bletchley—Cambridge route, but it did not survive the war.

There were many other experiments during the period with this new form of motive power, too numerous to go into detail here, but illustrated by a few more unusual views of interest.

Coaching Stock

A few words on coaching stock, a subject formerly very much bypassed, at least in comparison with the universal interest in the steam locomotive, but which has attracted an increasing amount of attention in recent years.

The changes and developments in passenger coaches on the main lines during the inter-war period lay principally in the gradual introduction of steel bodywork in place of the hitherto customary wood, usually with decorative panelling. Whilst the standards of comfort on main line coaches had already reached a very high degree on some railways, notably the Midland and the London & North Western, on others it still left much to be desired. Even such civilised amenities as lavatory facilities (in respect of which in these days railways have a decided advantage over the motor coach) were on some railways all too frequently conspicious by their absence, particularly on longer distance trains. The average standards of comfort provided on most local and suburban services were generally very poor, again with exceptions on such lines as the Midland. Six-wheeled coaches were still commonly met with, and four-wheelers were to be found here and there right into the 1930s, even, almost unbelievably, in the heart of the metropolis on the old North London Railway, and also in the Isle of Wight.* They were also to be found on two or three GWR branches up to 1938, but none lasted longer except for a few on the Burry Port & Gwendraeth Valley, in service until 1951, and some four-wheelers on the Caledonian, built as recently as 1921, running in the Edinburgh district until 1952. Gas lighting was giving way to electricity, but even this persisted until after World War II, notwithstanding some disastrous accidents involving fire which had occurred. In general, the appearance of new designs of coaching stock became progressively plainer, the handsome clerestory roofs once to be found on the Midland, North Eastern, Great Western, and several other railways, being definitely on the way out. As in most other spheres of life, fashions these days are much more austere, and utilitarian, and so with coaching stock. The picturesque embellishments of the Edwardian era

*In 1933, in fact, the LMS had 202 4-wheelers, and 759 6-wheelers, still in service, the GWR 540 and 204 respectively, the SR 84 and 405, while the LNER, the largest of all users of non-bogie stock 436 4-wheelers and no lesss than 2,834 6-wheelers, of which a not inconsiderable proportion was to be found on the Great Eastern suburban services.

which lasted into the 1930s are now no longer to be seen. The modern trend in favour of centre gangway coaches on main-line trains really began towards the end of the 1920s, at first mainly for excursion traffic and the like, for which they were no doubt more suitable. The comparative lack of privacy, however, coupled with the constant disturbance of passengers passing through, is nevertheless regarded nowadays by many as a distinctly retrograde step.

Restaurant cars had already become almost a standard feature on most of the chief expresses of the principal lines, apart from what later on became the constituents of the Southern group, before World War I, and after their temporary withdrawal under emergency conditions were restored as quickly as possible after the Armistice. They were developed on an increasing scale so that by 1938 there were no less than 895 in service. The use of Pullman cars also increased considerably after 1923, particularly on the SR and LNER.

A very much needed and welcome innovation in 1928 was the introduction of third-class sleeping cars, a luxury previously enjoyed only by those who were prepared to pay for them at first-class fares. No beds were provided, just a blanket and pillow, but one was at least assured of being able to lie full length in place of the previous hazard of having to sit up all night, or even, under the worst conditions, not having a seat at all. Four berths, two upper and two lower, were contained in each compartment; the sexes were segregated as far as possible, but if the distribution was uneven there was sometimes some interesting intermixing. The presence of four persons at any rate precluded the possibility of any untoward goings on!

Preservation

We may conclude with a few words on preservation, a subject very much in the limelight in recent years, but to which comparatively little attention had been given prior to World War II. The most laudable effort during the period was made by the LNER in setting up their fine museum at York, initially with about eight or nine engines, added to over the years so that there are now about a dozen.

The LMS put aside two or three former LNWR engines in Crewe paint shop, the most important being *Cornwall* and *Hardwicke*, and these have fortunately survived, whilst in Scotland the Caledonian single and the Jones goods No 103, the first 4-6-0 in Britain, were repainted in their old colours and kept at St Rollox. There was also the old Liverpool & Manchester engine *Lion*, unexpectedly discovered in a Liverpool dock on stationary boiler duty, and thanks to the LMS restored to working order, subsequently appearing at some exhibitions and latterly used for film work in *The Titfield Thunderbolt*. At Derby, too, what promised to be an interesting collection was started in 1929, with four Midland engines which were actually restored in their old liveries, and a North London 4-4-0T No 6445, which never got as far as this stage. One wonders whether it was by coincidence that all but (fortunately) the Midland single were broken up shortly after Mr Stanier arrived on the scene in 1932, remembering that he came from the GWR, which railway had a particularly bad reputation in this respect. True, they sent *City of Truro* to York, but one could not forget the earlier vandalism of 1906, when the two former broad-gauge engines *North Star* and *Lord of the Isles*, after having been kept at Swindon for a number of years, were quietly liquidated. Less known was a similar desecration which occurred in 1920, when a very fine example of a Sharp single, built in 1848 for the Shrewsbury & Chester Railway, a well-known type of the period, withdrawn in 1885 and which had been allowed to languish in Wolverhampton shed for thirty-five years, was suddenly cut up. A great tragedy, the comparatively small value as scrap metal and the few square yards of space it occupied being out of all proportion to the historic value it would have had today.

The Southern was not interested in preservation at this period, and it was left to private enterprise in the form of the Stephenson Locomotive Society, largely through the efforts of the late J. N. Maskelyne, which raised funds to purchase the first of Stroudley's 0-4-2 express engines, *Gladstone*, and have it restored, down to the last detail, to its original condition. This was the first venture of its kind, but was perhaps an indication of what was to come much later. The LNER gave it hospitality in York Museum.

A second attempt, unfortunately abortive, was a proposal to preserve the original Isle of Wight Beyer Peacock 2-4-0T *Ryde* of 1864, but after being stored at Eastleigh for three or four years, the second war intervened and it succumbed to the scrap metal drive. This was also responsible for another casualty in the form of North British Atlantic *Midlothian*, withdrawn in 1939, which the LNER had intended should be saved (the original GNR Atlantic *Henry Oakley* had meanwhile been restored and sent to York Museum).

The most enterprising project, however, again by the LNER, occurred towards the close of this 'between the wars' period, when they rooted out the Great Northern Stirling single No 1 from its retirement in York Museum in 1938 and ran it on a few excursions between London, Peterborough, and Cambridge with some suitably restored vintage 1888 six-wheeled stock, to the immense delight and enjoyment of the enthusiasts of the day. If, and I am afraid it is a very big 'if', but perhaps not entirely in the realms of fantasy, the present BR had the enterprise and will to perpetuate such an event (although the six-wheelers would no longer be available) the response would undoubtedly be staggering, and one could imagine that bookings would be such that it would only be possible to accommodate everyone by the running of many trips extending over weeks or even months! To travel again, not only behind a steam engine, but a hundred-year-old single-wheeler at that, an almost impossible ideal even forty years ago, would be an idea almost beyond conception in these bleak days. I well remember my own trip on one of these excursions, and how on our return to King's Cross after an exhilarating experience we were suddenly and rudely brought back to earth. It was the time of the Munich crisis; the placards read 'Germany mobilising', 'France mobilising', together with other grim forebodings of what was to come. In spite of Chamberlain's misplaced optimism it now seemed inevitable to most of us that we should have to go through it all again, for the second time in many of our lives, although as it turned out, there was to be another year's respite. These exploits of No 1 were of course of minor general importance, and nothing very spectacular occurred on the railways during the first nine months of 1939. History was, however, already beginning to repeat itself—engines scheduled for scrapping were laid aside and eventually put back into service, exactly as had happened a quarter of a century before.

At last in that fateful September the lights were literally to go out all over Europe. Things would never be quite the same again, and this was nowhere truer than in the case of the railways. To misquote and paraphrase the immortal words of Sir Winston Churchill: 'Those were their finest years'. In that period between the wars, from almost every angle, prosperity, enterprise (with the rather severe qualifications already spoken of), speed, and general standard of comfort and convenience, the railways had reached their maximum peak, and having surmounted the summit were about to begin the descent of their gradual but inevitable decline. The war undoubtedly slowed up this process to a large extent, in fact railways were once more to demonstrate their vital part both in the prosecution of the war itself and in the maintenance of communications within the country in general. It is in fact impossible to imagine how we could ever have survived or won the war without them. Considering all the difficulties, they did a wonderful job. This, perhaps, was one of the tiny silver linings which emerged from time to time from the otherwise almost persistent cloud which was to envelop us for nearly six years.

APPENDIX 1

1921 Railways Act

Consituents of newly formed groups effective in most cases from 1 January 1923.

LONDON MIDLAND & SCOTTISH RAILWAY

NOTE: The London & North Western and the Lancashire & Yorkshire had already amalgamated a year previously on 1 January 1922.

Constituent Companies

	route mileage
LNWR and L & YR (see above)	$2667\frac{1}{2}$
Midland	$2170\frac{3}{4}$
North Stafford	$220\frac{3}{4}$
Furness	158
Maryport & Carlisle	42
Caledonian	$1114\frac{1}{2}$
Glasgow & South Western	$493\frac{1}{2}$
Highland	506

Subsidiary Companies

Independently operated

	Cleator & Workington (partially worked by Furness Ry.)	$30\frac{1}{2}$
	Knott End	$11\frac{1}{2}$
	North London (managed by LNWR)	16
	Stratford-on-Avon & Midland Jn.	$67\frac{1}{2}$
	Wirral	$13\frac{3}{4}$

Independent lines using rolling stock of other Companies

	Cockermouth Keswick & Penrith (LNWR) (NER)	$30\frac{3}{4}$

Companies originally leased to or worked by

LNWR	Charnwood Forest	$10\frac{1}{2}$
	Harborne	$2\frac{1}{2}$
	Mold & Denbigh Junction	15
	Shropshire Union Railways & Canal (partly with the GWR)	$29\frac{1}{4}$
L & YR	Dearne Valley	21
MR	Tottenham & Forest Gate	6
	Yorkshire Dales (Skipton to Grassington)	9
CR	Arbroath & Forfar	$14\frac{3}{4}$
	Brechin & Edzell District	$6\frac{1}{4}$
	Callander & Oban	$99\frac{3}{4}$
	Dundee & Newtyle	$14\frac{1}{2}$
	Killin	$5\frac{1}{4}$
	Lanarkshire & Ayrshire	$36\frac{1}{4}$
	Solway Junction	$12\frac{1}{4}$
HR	Dornoch Light	$7\frac{3}{4}$
	Wick & Lybster Light	$13\frac{1}{2}$
NSR	Leek & Manifold (narrow gauge)	$8\frac{1}{4}$

Sundry component companies

North & South Western Junction (LNWR, Midland and North London)	$5\frac{1}{4}$
Portpatrick & Wigtownshire Jt. (Glasgow & South Western, Caledonian, LNWR, and Midland)	$82\frac{1}{4}$

Subsidiary companies (Irish Lines)

Dundalk Newry & Greenore (LNWR)	$26\frac{1}{2}$
Northern Counties Committee (Midland)	$265\frac{1}{4}$

Joint lines coming wholly within the LMS

Ashby & Nuneaton (LNWR and Midland)	$29\frac{1}{4}$
Enderby (LNWR and Midland)	$2\frac{3}{4}$
Preston & Wyre (LNWR and L & YR)	46
Preston and Longridge (LNWR and L & YR)	8
Lancashire Union (LNWR and L & YR)	$12\frac{3}{4}$
North Union (LNWR and L & YR)	$6\frac{1}{2}$
Furness & Midland (FR and MR)	$9\frac{3}{4}$
Whitehaven Cleator & Egremont (LNWR and Furness)	35
Glasgow Barrhead & Kilmarnock (CR and GSWR)	$29\frac{3}{4}$
Glasgow & Paisley (CR and GSWR)	$14\frac{1}{4}$
Carlisle Citadel (LNWR and Caledonian)—and Goods traffic Joint Committee	

LONDON & NORTH EASTERN RAILWAY

NOTE: The Hull & Barnsley Railway had been absorbed by the North Eastern on 1 April 1922.

Constituent Companies

	route mileage
North Eastern	1757¾
Great Northern	1051¼
Great Eastern	1191¼
Great Central	852½
Hull & Barnsley	106½
North British	1378
Great North of Scotland	334½

Subsidiary Companies

Independently Operated

	Colne Valley & Halstead	19
	Mid-Suffolk Light	19½
	East & West Yorkshire Union	9¼

Companies originally leased to or worked by

NER	Brackenhill Light	—
	Forcett	5½
	Great North of England, Clarence & Hartlepool Junction	6¾
GCR	Humber Commercial Railway & Dock	—
	Mansfield	10
	North Lindsey Light	12
	Seaforth & Sefton Junction	—
	Sheffield District	4¼
GER	London & Blackwall	6
GNR	East Lincolnshire Railway	47½
	Horncastle	7½
	Nottingham & Grantham Railway & Canal	23
	Nottingham Suburban	4
	Stamford & Essendine	4
NER	Edinburgh & Bathgate	10¼
	Forth & Clyde Junction	30½
	Gifford & Garvald	9¼
	Kilsyth & Bonnybridge (worked jointly with CR)	8½
	Lauder Light	10¼
	Newburgh & North Fife	13¼

Originally leased to or worked by the GNR and GCR

Nottingham Joint Station Committee	—
West Riding Railway Committee	32½

Joint lines now coming wholly within the LNER

GN & GE Joint	123
Hull & Barnsley & Great Central Jt.	25¾

GREAT WESTERN RAILWAY

Constituent Companies

(amalgamated as from 1 January 1922)

	route mileage
Great Western	3005
Barry	68
Cambrian	295¼
Cardiff	11¾
Rhymney	51
Taff Vale	124½
Alexandra Docks & Railway (Newport and South Wales)	10¼

Subsidiary Companies

Independently operated

Brecon & Merthyr (Absorbed 1 July 1922)	59¾
Burry Port & Gwendraeth Valley (Absorbed 1 July 1922)	21
Cleobury Mortimer & Ditton Priors (Absorbed 1 Jan. 1922)	12
Llanelly & Mynydd Mawr (Absorbed 1 Jan. 1923)	13
Midland & South Western Junction (Absorbed 1 July 1923)	63¼
Neath & Brecon (Absorbed 1 July 1922)	40

Semi-independent Companies—worked by GWR *but possessing independent rolling stock, etc.*

Port Talbot Railways & Docks (Absorbed 1 Jan. 1922)	35
Rhondda & Swansea Bay (Absorbed 1 Jan. 1922)	29
South Wales Mineral (Absorbed 1 Jan. 1923)	13

Companies originally leased to or worked by

GWR	Didcot Newbury & Southampton	42¾
	Exeter	8¾
	Forest of Dean Central	5
	Gwendraeth Valley (Absorbed 1 Jan. 1923)	3
	Lampeter Aberayron & New Quay Light	12
	Liskeard & Looe	9
	Princetown	10½
	Ross & Monmouth	12½
	Teign Valley	7¾
	West Somerset	14½
	Swansea Harbour Trust (dock line) Absorbed 1 July 1923)	
	Powlesland & Mason (dock line) (Absorbed 1 Jan. 1924)	
TAFF VALE		
	Penarth Extension	1¼
	Penarth Harbour, Docks & Rly	9¼
CAMBRIAN		
	Mawddy	6¾
	Van	6¾
	Welshpool & Llanfair Light	9¼
	Vale of Rheidol	11¾
	Wrexham & Ellesmere	12¾
	Tanat Valley	16
PORT TALBOT RAILWAY & DOCKS		
	South Wales Mineral (see above) (Absorbed 1 Jan. 1923)	13
BARRY RAILWAY		
	Vale of Glamorgan	20¾

Joint lines now coming wholly in GWR

Quakers Yard & Merthyr (GWR & Rhymney)	6
Taff Bargoed (GWR & Rhymney)	11

SOUTHERN RAILWAY

The Lynton & Barnstaple narrow-gauge line was absorbed by the LSWR, although not included in the 1921 Railways Act.

Constituent Companies

	route mileage
London and South Western Railway, including Lynton and Barnstaple	19¼ + 1020½ = 1039¾
London Brighton & South Coast	457¼
London Chatham & Dover South Eastern (South Eastern & Chatham Managing Committee)	637¾

Subsidiary Companies

Independently Operated

Freshwater Yarmouth & Newport	12
Isle of Wight	15¼
Isle of Wight Central	28½
Bere Alston & Callington section of Plymouth Devonport & SW Junction	9¾

JOINT LINES NOT COMING WHOLLY WITHIN ANY ONE OF THE NEWLY FORMED GROUPS

These lines nominally retained their independent status until Nationalisation on 1 January 1948, although in effect they were usually worked as part of the system by one of the owning partners. Exceptions to this pattern were two of the largest Joint Railways, the Midland & Great Northern Joint and the Somerset & Dorset, which retained all the outward characteristics of independent railways for many years, including the provision of their own distinctive locomotives and rolling stock. The Cheshire Lines also had its separate coaching stock lettered CLC right up to nationalisation, although its locomotives had always been supplied by the parent Companies, principally the GCR.

Joint lines between the newly formed LMS and LNER

Not included under the provision of the Railways Act of 1921 were the Metropolitan and Metropolitan District, which, along with the underground systems of London, were later all to be combined under the London Passenger Transport Board, created in 1933. A complication of the 1923 grouping, however, arose in the fact that certain of the Metropolitan lines were already jointly owned with some of the main-line companies, and these had to be brought within the scope of the 1921 Railways Act. The details are summarised as under:

Mention might also be made at this point of the Joint Watford Extension, newly opened in 1925, jointly between the Metropolitan and what was now the LNER, but this was of course a post-grouping development.

OTHER LIGHT AND INDEPENDENT PASSENGER RAILWAYS NOT INCLUDED IN THE GROUPING UNDER THE 1921 RAILWAYS ACT

All Irish railways, apart from those owned or partly owned by English Companies (viz, Northern Counties Committee, Dundalk, Newry & Greenore, and County Donegal).

Metropolitan; Metropolitan District and London Underground lines; Mersey; Liverpool Overhead; Isle of Man; Manx Electric; Jersey; Jersey Eastern; Campbeltown & Machrihanish; South Shields, Marsden & Whitburn; North Sunderland; Easingwold; Nidd Valley Light; Stocksbridge; Ravenglass & Eskdale; Festiniog; Welsh Highland; Snowdon Mountain; Talyllyn; Shropshire & Montgomeryshire; Bishops Castle; Glyn Valley; Snailbeach District; Swansea & Mumbles; Weston Clevedon & Portishead; West Sussex (Selsey Tramway); Kent & East Sussex; East Kent; Wantage Tramway; Southwold; Rye & Camber; Corringham Light; Sand Hutton; Manchester Ship Canal; Mersey Docks & Harbour Board; Port of London Authority; Felixstowe Dock & Railway; Kings Lynn Dock & Railway.

APPENDIX 2

A Brief Diary of the More Important and Interesting Events in the Period Between the Wars

1918
11 Nov: Armistice between the Allies and Germany signed in dining car No 2419 of Wagons Lits attached to Marshall Foch's train in Compeigne Forest

1919
1 Jan.: Wartime regulation under DORA (Defence of Realm Act) regarding prohibition of taking of railway photographs lifted.
3 Feb.: Folkestone-Boulogne passenger service resumed
25 Feb.: GER Continental service via Parkeston Quay resumed.
May: Restoration of LBSC Southern Belle all-Pullman train
14 May: Service at St Paul's Cathedral 'In memory of the railwaymen of Great Britain and Ireland who died in the service of their country'. (In all 18,957 railway employees of all grades had given their lives.)
1 June: Newhaven-Dieppe service resumed.
16 June: Pullman cars restored on Folkestone and Kent Coast Expresses, SE & CR
13 Aug.: Act authorises setting up of Ministry of Transport from appointed date to be announced
23 Sept.: Ministry of Transport established under Act of 13 August and transfer to it of all transport powers of Board of Trade and other Government departments
27 Sept.-5 Oct.: Railway strike

1920
1 Jan.: Control of railways passes to Ministry of Transport. During the year there was much discussion on the future of the railways, including suggestions of nationalisation. The projected grouping produced a number of proposals and counter proposals
8 Jan.: Dover-Calais service resumed
14 May: Hull-Zeebrugge service resumed, NER and L & YR
12 July: Inauguration of intensive 'Jazz' suburban service out of Liverpool Street, GER
26 Sept.: Metropolitan District Railway decontrolled under special act.
3 Oct.: First section of Feltham LSWR Concentration Yard brought into use. 'Hump' shunting commenced on 1 May 1921
24 Dec.: Period excursion tickets restored for Christmas holiday

1921
26 Jan.: Collision on single line between Abermule and Newtown, Cambrian Railways, due to irregular signalling (14 killed)
1 Apr.-3 July: Coal strike. The threatened rail strike did not materialise, but shortage of coal involved reduction of services
11 July: Summer timetable, with improved services on many railways
25 July: Through Liverpool-Harwich continental service resumed
15 Aug.: Railways decontrolled as from midnight 15/16 Aug.
19 Aug.: Railways Act received royal assent
3 Oct.: Inauguration of through Aberdeen-Penzance train, worked over the lines of the NBR, NER, GCR and GWR. London-Birmingham best trains reduced to two hours, and to Leeds, Manchester, and Liverpool, four hours. Most railways reverted to pre-war timings
31 Oct.: New up side marshalling yard and 'hump' shunting at Llandilo Junction GWR brought into use

1922
1 Jan.: Amalgamation of LNWR and L & YR. Hull & Barnsley taken over by NER. Several railways absorbed by GWR (See Appendix 1)
15 June: Gravesend-Rotterdam service introduced SE & CR
10 July: NER reinstated pre-war timing of forty-three minutes for the forty-four miles Darlington-York, the fastest publicly advertised start to stop booking in the British Isles
July: LNWR completed large-scale widening of the line between Chalk Farm and Kensal Green, including new burrowing junctions. Electric trains commenced running into Euston on 10 July

1923
1 Jan.: Establishment of the four new groups under the Railways Act of 1921. For full details see Appendix 1
1 June: Welsh Highland Railway opened, connecting Portmadoc with the former North Wales Narrow Gauge Railway
1 July: Midland & South Western Junction Railway taken over by GWR. The last independent railway to be absorbed into the grouping

9 July: GWR introduced a Cheltenham-Paddington express train timed at 61·8 mph, just beating the record previously held by the NER
LNER introduced all-Pullman train to Harrogate
17 Sept.: Fishguard-Rosslare service resumed
1 Oct.: Abolition of second-class accommodation on SE & CR (apart from Continental boat trains)

1924
24 April: Inauguration of Harwich-Zeebrugge train ferry
13 Sept.: Closure of Listowel & Ballybunion Railway, Ireland's unique Lartigue mono-rail system

1924/25
Summer months: Wembley Exhibition. The four groups combined in a large railway stand in the Palace of Engineering, with representative locomotives and other exhibits

1925
1 Jan.: All railways in the Irish Free State amalgamated as the Great Southern Railways.
New GWR line west of Wolverhampton serving Himley and other villages opened for goods traffic (passengers on 11 May)
30 Jan.: Train blown off viaduct in gale at Owencarrow, Letterkenny & Burtonport Extension Railway
1-3 July: Centenary of Stockton & Darlington Railway celebrations held at Darlington
12 July: First section of SE & CR to be electrified, Victoria and Holborn Viaduct-Orpington and Orpington-Crystal Palace
20 July: Totton Hythe & Fawley Railway opened
27 July: North Devon & Cornwall Junction Railway opened.
1 Oct.: Abolition of second-class accommodation on NLR, Broad Street-Poplar services
2 Nov.: New branch to Watford opened by Metropolitan and LNER

1926
4-14 May: General strike. Some railway services maintained by volunteers
2 July: New lines in Ramsgate area opened by SR with closure of some others
12 Sept.: SR introduced Golden Arrow all-Pullman continental boat train

1927
15 May: Tilbury-Dunkirk Continental service inaugurated by LMS
24 May: LBSC *Gladstone* restored by Stephenson Locomotive Society left Battersea for York Museum. First instance of a privately sponsored preservation scheme
11 July: Introduction of regular non-stop trains by LMS between Euston and Carnforth and by LNER King's Cross-Newcastle (see also 26 Sept.)
Aug.: Parking of motor cars at stations introduced by LMS and GWR. Charge 1s per day (the LNER followed in 1928)
24 Aug.: Derailment at Sevenoaks caused by unstable locomotive allied with poor condition of track and ballast (13 killed)
Sept.: GWR 6000 *King George V* left England for exhibition at Baltimore USA
26 Sept.: Cornish Riviera speeded up to four hours between Paddington and Plymouth
Carnforth stop omitted (see 11 July) and non-stop extended to Carlisle
19 Oct.: Conveyance of milk in glass-lined tanks of 2,000 and 3,000 gallons capacity instead of in churns introduced by GWR and LMS in collaboration with United Dairies Ltd. (The LNER followed on 13 December 1928)

1928
Jan.: Adoption of yellow arms and lights for distant signals by all companies. The changeover was generally completed by March 1931
27 Apr.: LMS anticipated LNER by running two trains non-stop from Euston to Glasgow and Edinburgh (on one occasion only)
1 May: Introduction by LNER of non-stop running between King's Cross and Edinburgh. Longest regular non-stop run in the world.
All-Pullman Queen of Scots introduced by LNER between London and Edinburgh and Glasgow. First all steel car trains
19 Aug.: Spectacular filming of *The Wrecker* depicting a level-crossing collision between a train and a lorry. Staged on the disused Basingstoke-Alton track, the engine being a SE & CR Stirling 4-4-0 No A148 with dummy driver on footplate and train of SE & CR coaches
24 Sept.: Introduction of third-class sleepers by LMS, LNER and GWR
13 Oct.: Double collision and fire at Charfield LMS (17 killed, including two children 'unclaimed' and buried in Charfield churchyard). The collision involved three trains, two LMS and one GWR

1929
May: Railway investment in larger motor omnibus companies commenced and transfer to them of some railway-owned bus services. Eventually all such services were transferred to these 'associated' companies
7 July: First portion of new Wimbledon & Sutton Railway as far as South Merton opened
21 Sept.: Last LB & SCR overhead electric left Victoria for Coulsdon 12.30 a.m.

1929-1931
GWR introduced automatic train control over many of its principal main lines

1930
1 Jan.: Somerset & Dorset Joint Railway locos absorbed into LMS stock
5 Jan.: Completion of Wimbledon-Sutton line
1 July: Separate management of S & DJR abolished. Operating department transferred to LMS and civil engineering to SR
4 Aug.: Corris Railway taken over by GWR
13-20 Sept.: Centenary celebrations of the Liverpool & Manchester railway held at Wavertree Park, Liverpool

1931
1 Jan.: Canterbury & Whitstable, the oldest part of the SR, closed for passenger traffic after 100 years of operation
22 Mar.: Collision at Leighton Buzzard. Driver's view of signals obscured by steam drifting over boiler of a Royal Scot, a fault to which these engines and some others of modern type were particularly prone. Eventually alleviated to some extent by the fitting of deflector plates alongside the smokebox
8 May: Electrification of Manchester South Junction and Altrincham Railways, first application of 1,500 volts dc overhead system recommended by the WEIR report for all future electrifications.
5 July: First diesel railcar in the British Isles brought into service by County Donegal Railway in Ireland
21 July: LMS adopted upper-quadrant signals as standard. First one was provided at Bedford St Johns station
30 Aug.: LMS commenced programme of installing 'intermediate' and 'advanced' section signals to replace small intermediate block posts. The first installation was at Dunkirk box, between Mollington and Capenhurst

1932

Apr-June: LMS ran experimental ro-rail bus, designed to be capable of running either on rail or road between their Welcombe Hotel, Stratford-on-Avon, and Blisworth, over former SMJ Railway

14 May: All Hallows branch passenger services commenced by SR (goods traffic had been in operation since 1 March)

17 July: Brighton electrification inaugurated as far as Three Bridges

10 Dec.: Metropolitan Railway Stanmore branch opened. This year was the centenary of the Leicester & Swannington Railway, the oldest section of the LMS

1933

1 Jan.: SR Brighton and Worthing electrification completed. The first large-scale application of main line electric traction in Great Britain. The all Pullman Southern Belle, now an electric multiple unit, renamed Brighton Belle

11 Apr.: First aeroplane service to be operated by a British railway, between Cardiff and Plymouth; machine supplied by Imperial Airways and painted in GWR colours

1 June: Registered transits of goods traffic introduced by all the main-line companies. Side lights on passenger trains discontinued by all main-line companies

16 June: First rail cruise, a six-day tour of Scotland from London, inaugurated by the LNER, covering 1,873 miles. The train consisted of six first-class sleepers, two daytime coaches, restaurant car, buffet car, etc

1 July: Establishment of London Passenger Transport Board, comprising the Metropolitan and Metropolitan District Railways, all Underground lines, trams and buses, both those operated by the London General Omnibus Company and private owners

26 July: Completion of Southampton Docks extension by opening of King George V Graving Dock

During 1933: LMS No 6100 *Royal Scot* (actually No 6152, built at Derby in 1930) was sent to America for exhibition at Chicago, after which it covered 11,194 miles touring the United States and Canada before being returned to England

1934

12 Mar.: Leek & Manifold Valley Light Railway, the only LMS narrow gauge line, closed

21 July: The last of Brunel's numerous timber viaducts in Cornwall, at Collegewood, on the Falmouth branch, was taken out of service and replaced by a new stone bridge

1935

7 Jan.: Electric traction discontinued on NER Shildon line

7 July: Brighton line electrification extended to Eastbourne and Hastings

31 Aug.: Centenary of incorporation of GWR

27 Sept.: 112½ mph attained by new Gresley streamlined Pacific on trial

30 Sept.: The Silver Jubilee, Britain's first streamlined train, commenced regular service between London and Newcastle, 268¼ miles in four hours
Lynton & Barnstaple Railway, the SR's only narrow-gauge line, closed

2 Dec.: Closure of the Brill branch (originally the Oxford & Aylesbury Tramway), that curious rural outpost of London's busy Metropolitan system

1936

1 Oct.: Operation and maintenance of Midland & Great Northern Joint Railway transferred to LNER. Locomotives absorbed into LNER stock

14 Oct.: First through train between London and Paris by the newly opened Dover-Dunkirk ferry

16/17 Nov.: High-speed test trains between Euston and Glasgow with Pacific 6201 *Princess Elizabeth*. The 401½ miles covered in 353 minutes in the down direction and 344 minutes up

1937

29 June: Trial run of LMS streamlined train Coronation Scot. Maximum speed 114 mph attained

5 July: Commencement of LMS Coronation Scot and LNER Coronation services to Glasgow and Edinburgh

27 Sept.: LNER West Riding streamlined train King's Cross-Leeds and Bradford

1 Nov.: Working of Metropolitan trains between Rickmansworth and Aylesbury handed over to LNER, which absorbed London Transport 'main line' locomotives into its own stock. LT retained some engines for its own use on departmental duties

31 Dec.: Abolition of second class on GNR and GER suburban trains, also LMS trains from Broad Street over LNER suburban routes. Apart from certain Continental services, this was the end of pure second-class accommodation, as distinct from the modern description of the old third class

1938

2 May: Acceleration of LMS Royal Scot to seven hours to Glasgow and seven hours five minutes to Edinburgh, by separate trains calling at Carlisle. The rival Flying Scotsman of the LNER reached Edinburgh in seven hours, but over a route seven miles shorter than the LMS. Also the 5.25 pm Liverpool-Euston was timed for three and a quarter hours, the 158 miles from Crewe being run in 148 minutes (64 mph). This train was often worked by the experimental turbine locomotive No 6202

30 June: First run by GNR Stirling 4-2-2 No 1 brought out from York Museum. Several subsequent trips were made, between King's Cross and Peterborough or Cambridge

3 July: LNER Pacific No 4468 *Mallard* attained 126 mph, the highest fully authenticated speed in the world with steam

19-25 Sept.: Centenary of London & Birmingham Railway. Exhibition of locos and rolling stock at Euston station, including 0-4-2 *Lion*, 2-2-2 *Cornwall*, FR *Coppernob*, GV 4-4-0 No 25348 *Coronation*, and Pacific 6225 *Duchess of Gloucester*

1939

2 Jan.: Closure of the Wanlockhead branch in Scotland transferred to the distinction of Great Britain's highest standard-gauge passenger summit of 1,498 feet above sea level to the better known 1,484 feet at Druimuachdar on the old Highland Railway

28 May: Chessington branch completed by SR, the last standard-gauge completely new railway, apart from London Underground extensions, various diversions, new loops, and so on, in the country

1 Sept.: Ministry of Transport order takes control of main-line railways, joint lines, and various light railways. Large-scale evacuation by railways of women and children from London and other large centres of population. The numbers moved totalled over a quarter of a million in 3823 special trains, of which over 600,000 were from London

3 Sept.: WAR DECLARED BY GREAT BRITAIN AND FRANCE AGAINST GERMANY

The Immediate Post-War Years

The year 1919 saw the repatriation of many locomotives which had served in France during the war years, and many of them, strangers to south England, such as Caledonian and North British 0-6-0s, were seen passing through London on their way home.

The Midland had sent some eighty of Kirtley's double-framed 0-6-0s, veterans of the early 1870s, one of which was captured by the Germans. All returned safely to put in many further years of service. Here is No 2727, with the initials of the Railway Operating Department, at Derby on 1 January 1920, after its return.

Some of the smaller railways also made their contributions to the war effort, and this view shows an old Rhymney 0-6-0ST, one of ten built by Messrs Sharp Stewart & Co in 1872, RR Nos 23-32. Three of them, Nos 24, 26, and 28, were sold to the War Department in 1916 and became WD Nos 100-2, being sent to Catterick Camp in Yorkshire, where they worked during the war. Later No 101 was transferred to the WD depot at Longmoor, Hants, and this view shows it at Strawberry Hill, LSWR, on 31 December 1921 en route.

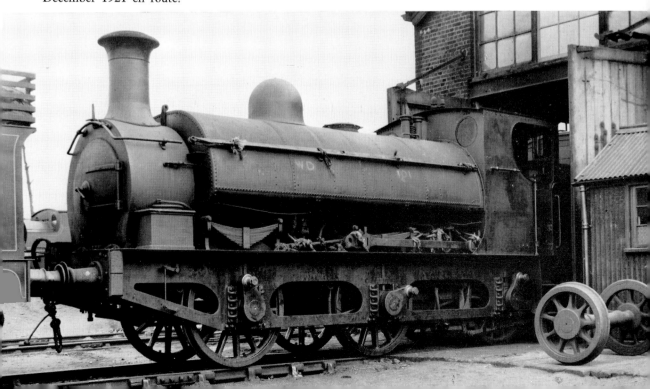

Engines withdrawn from traffic on the LSWR during the war years, chiefly Adams 4-4-2Ts, displaced by the London electrification, together with other engines found unfit for further service, gradually accumulated in the works yard at Eastleigh, as no labour could be spared for breaking them up. By 1920 there were over a hundred of them in a paradise for the young 'spotter' of those days, although this was long before that somewhat dubious term—often now annoyingly applied to genuine and mature enthusiasts—had been thought up. This view taken on 14 April 1922, shows No 0419 together with several others of the class lying in the graveyard. This one was not finally cut up until November 1923.

Engines which had been retained during the war years to help with the locomotive shortage began to be laid aside when conditions became easier. Amongst these were the Johnson singles of the Midland, many of which had been employed on such unsuitable duties as piloting goods trains. Here is a group of them at Kentish Town in 1921, foremost being No 685, the *Princess of Wales* herself, probably the most famous of the class.

34

The North British had provided twenty-four of Holmes C class 0-6-0s (later LNER J36) for service in France, and on return they were given suitable commemorative names, such as No 646 *Somme*. Most of them retained these for the rest of their existence (nearly all lasted well into BR days). The naming of goods engines has always been rare in Great Britain, although it was normal practice at one time on the Midland Great Western and Great Northern Railways of Ireland.

Three other railways gave names in honour of their fallen employees, each with suitable inscriptions or commemorative plaques. Great Central Lord Faringdon class No 1165 was named *Valour*, LBSC 4-6-4T No 333 (later rebuilt as 4-6-0) *Remembrance*, and LNWR Claughton class, appropriately numbered 1914, was *Patriot*.

Many railways had adopted simplified and more economical styles of painting during the war years. The Great Northern engines, except for the Atlantics, appeared in grey lined out with a single white band, exemplified here by one of Ivatt's handsome suburban tanks at King's Cross in 1921.

The prolonged miners' strikes of 1921 and 1926 (the latter coinciding with the ten days general strike) resulted in the conversion of some engines by several railways to burn oil fuel, although the number was too small to result in any appreciable benefit. Here is a Midland Johnson class 3 4-4-0, at that time unsuperheated, so fitted, at Derby in 1921.

One of the first visible results of the grouping in 1923 was the appearance of the locomotives and rolling stock in new styles of painting, indicating the ownership of the new railway. The two large groups, the LMS in particular (the LNWR section excepted) seemed especially anxious to eradicate the identity of the former railways, even to the extent of casting new works plates, as seen in this illustration, a somewhat pointless exercise. This Highland engine had been built long before the new organisation had been even remotely thought of.

The Southern was not quite so well off the mark and it was several months before a new style was decided upon, during which time engines continued to be repainted with the old companies' styles.

The Great Western was unaffected, except that the engines it absorbed were re-numbered into its own stock list and acquired number plates of standard GWR pattern.

The London Midland & Scottish Railway

The LMS quickly decided on the lovely Midland lake livery, introduced by Johnson in the 1880s, for its passenger locomotives and coaching stock. This early example shows the last remaining Lancashire & Yorkshire 2-4-0, then working as an officers' inspection unit, in the first style, with the initials LMS on the cabside, soon to be replaced by the new crest, best seen in the illustration of No 14199 (next page). The new colour did not go down at all well with Crewe, who for several years obstinately refused to apply it on a general scale, or even to renumber their engines in accordance with the newly drawn up scheme, under which they were allocated the block 5000-9999. They thought they ought to have come first, and until at least 1928 persisted in turning out many of their engines from Crewe Works in LNWR guise.

The standard livery was, however, strictly adhered to in Scotland; the Highland engines in particular looked very fine after their former drab unlined green, and for the first few years they were kept in immaculate condition. Whether by coincidence or otherwise, it happened that a general deterioration set in after 1928, when only the largest express types continued to be honoured with red livery, and this did not apply to any Highland classes. Henceforth the standard of cleanliness fell from being among the highest in the country to the very lowest, degenerating to the general state of griminess to which we became all too accustomed in more recent years.

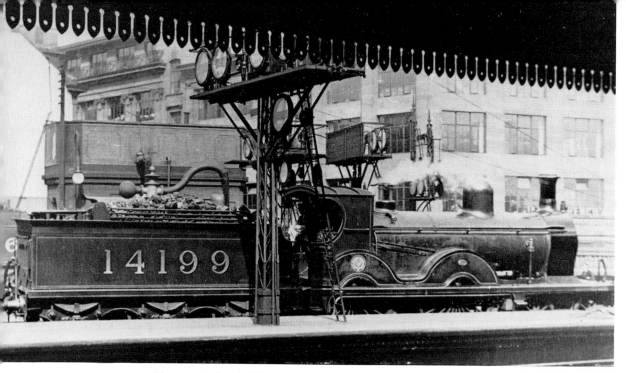

Glasgow & South Western engines also looked very well in their new guise, although the loss of the very pleasant rich green with brown framing—not unlike that of the old Great Central—was regretted by many.

Although of pure Caledonian design, this engine was one of a final batch of ten built in 1925. It is seen here at Kentish Town in 1927, when it was sent south for trials on the Midland suburban services, but nothing permanent resulted from this experiment. A Lancashire & Yorkshire 2-4-2T was also tried out. Something more powerful than the Johnson 0-4-4Ts was becoming necessary, and a few of the rather ungainly Deeley 0-6-4Ts and some of the LT & SR 4-6-4Ts provided a temporary stop gap until the appearance of the very successful Fowler 2-6-4Ts a year or two later (see next illustration). Another rather curious and not very successful experiment of this nature was the transfer of two or three North Stafford 2-4-0Ts to the Poplar service on the North London Railway.

The answer to the problem of the St Pancras suburban traffic came in 1928 with the appearance of Fowler's design of 2-6-4T. An up train seen here near Elstree in 1931. This basic design was developed by Stanier and used in large numbers all over the LMS system in later years, a three-cylinder variety being designed for use over the LT & S section.

The story of the LNWR suburban service at this period ran on much the same lines. Until the appearance of the Fowler tanks the shorter runs to Tring were mainly hauled by Whale's 4-4-2Ts, one of which is seen here passing Camden in 1933. It is regretted that the intriguing appearance of the coaching stock cannot be identified in detail. Note in the background, the roof of the original London & Birmingham engine roundhouse, which still stands to this day, although used for other purposes.

Out of the many thousands of locomotives inherited from the old companies by the new groups, the oldest of all was this veteran of 1848, built originally by the long defunct firm of Messrs E. B. Wilson & Co as a 2-2-2 tender engine and rebuilt as a 0-6-0WT in 1872. Midland engines were of sturdy, well-built construction, and large numbers of them enjoyed very long lives. It became LMS No 1605, to make way for a North Stafford 0-6-0T before being broken up in January 1924. With a few exceptions such as this, Midland engines retained their existing numbers in the new renumbering scheme which was drawn up to include all of the former Companies' engines which now came into the LMS.

The last users of the steam rail motor car, which enjoyed brief popularity in the early 1900s, were the GWR and L & YR; there was also one LNWR example. Lancashire & Yorkshire car No 10616 is seen here at Wakefield in 1933 with the Dearne Valley branch train.

A typical Midland light express of the 1930s. Up Nottingham express via Melton Mowbray running into Manton behind one of the five original Johnson compound 4-4-0s, as subsequently rebuilt by Deeley.

Llandudno-Birmingham express leaving Colwyn Bay about 1929, with Precursor class 4-4-0 No 5221 *Vizier* in original condition.

Highland Railway Farther North express entering The Mound, junction for the Dornoch branch, in 1928, headed by No 14676 *Ballindalloch Castle*.

The depression years. A scene at Cricklewood in May 1931, consisting of a row of Midland 0-6-0Ts, headed by No 1793, laid off temporarily through lack of work. A sight never before encountered, although it was to become common in more recent years through other causes.

A typical freight train on the Midland Railway, this one in pregrouping years, showing Johnson 0-6-0s Nos 3552 and 2904 near Kegworth. Owing to its small-engine policy, double heading on the MR remained the rule rather than the exception, particularly as regards goods trains.

The rising cost of wages, hitherto of comparatively less importance, made the elimination of double heading of increasing urgency, and in 1927 the LMS decided to experiment with three Garratt locomotives, a type already successfully used abroad, but only so far in Britain by Gresley's solitary engine for the Worsboro' incline, and one or two small industrial locomotives. Thirty more followed in 1930, but these were destined to be the only large-scale application of the design in this country.

No 4999, one of the original engines, seen here at Hendon in 1928. All except two were later fitted with revolving coal bunkers, to alleviate the fireman's arduous task in what boiled down to, or perhaps more literally boiled UP to supplying steam for two engines simultaneously! The problem was not finally solved until the appearance of Stanier's class 8 2-8-0s in 1935.

In 1933 the *Royal Scot*, not the original engine, but No 6152, renumbered 6100 and renamed, crossed the Atlantic, and made an extensive tour on the railways of both the United States and Canada. It is seen here alongside the 'Broadway Limited' express.

The experimental compound No 6399 *Fury*, built at Derby in 1932, was a three-cylinder machine with a boiler pressure of no less than 900 lb per square inch. Unfortunately on its first trials one of the tubes burst, killing an inspector on the footplate. Further tests were made, but the engine never ran in ordinary service, and it was rebuilt on conventional lines in 1935, reappearing at No 6170 *British Legion*.

A number of experimental condensing and turbine steam locomotives were tried out at various times between the wars, amongst which was a 2-6-6-2 Ramsay turbine electric, which worked trials on the NER and L & YR during 1921. There was also a Swedish designed Ljungstrom turbine condensing engine built under licence by Messrs Beyer Peacock & Co in 1926 and which worked for a considerable time on the Midland section of the LMS. It was found to be capable of running 500 miles without taking water. Some trouble was encountered in tunnels, owing to soot getting into the condensers and blocking the passages between the tubes. The exhaust steam from the turbine passed via a reservoir into the condenser. The wheel arrangement is not easy to specify under the Whyte system, and can only rather clumsily be described as a 10-6-4, or possibly 4-6-6-4, but only the third group of wheels constituted the drivers. Seen here at St Pancras with a Midland express train in 1928.

Since before World War I and up to quite recent times the War Department has maintained a large centre at Longmoor, Hants, where army personnel were given extensive training in railway operation. This was of course increased on a larger scale during the actual periods of the two wars, but it also maintained a regular routine part of service training during peace time. This view shows an officers' staff train at Bordon in 1934, the engine being one of two LNWR Webb 2-4-2Ts which were amongst a very miscellaneous collection to be found there at that time. This one, *Earl Roberts*, had been LMS 6610. The other, *Earl Haig*, was late 6613. These had originally been LNWR 608 and 658. Built at Crewe in 1891, they survived to World War II.

The London & North Eastern Railway

Taken shortly after the grouping, this handsome GCR Robinson 4-6-2T carries the initials of the new company, whilst still retaining Great Central livery and number plate. Under the renumbering scheme it later became No 5448.

The standard livery adopted for passenger engines was Great Northern green, but with black framing in lieu of brown. Numbers were at first carried on the tender, a style inherited from the Midland and now adopted not only by the LMS and LNER, but also the Southern. In 1928, however, the two large railways reverted to the more normal practice of placing the number on the cabside, as it was found that confusion was likely to arise when engines temporarily exchanged tenders for any reason.

This view shows a GCR Pollitt 4-4-0 at Trafford Park in 1926. The general similarity to the G & SWR 4-4-0s mentioned on page 9 will be noted by comparison with the illustration on page 38.

A typical North Eastern express about 1927, picturesque but perhaps not quite in keeping with more recent ideas and the Clean Air Act! The engine is one of the handsome Worsdell R class (later D20) of 1899, No 708, and is seen leaving Scarborough.

One of the later modified Great Eastern Claud Hamilton 4-4-0s, actually built in 1923 just after the grouping. Seen here on a Southend train near Billericay in 1936.

Pleasant scene on the North Eastern at Kirby Stephen in 1935. Two J21 class 0-6-0s, which worked most of the passenger traffic, are seen here, Nos 996 and 147, whilst a smaller wheeled J25 freight engine is in the distance. Note the clerestory stock, at that time a common sight on the North Eastern. This very attractive line is now unfortunately completely closed and abandoned.

Gresley's 'hush hush' engine of 1929, built under conditions of great secrecy. Its unusual features comprised a water-tube boiler and a working pressure of 450 lb per square inch. It was a compound, with two high- and two low-pressure cylinders, and was considerably more successful than the LMS high-pressure locomotive (page 44). Nevertheless it was eventually rebuilt on the lines of the A4 Pacifics, albeit that this was a 4-6-4 engine, and incidentally Britain's most powerful passenger locomotive.

A typical stretch of the East Coast main line, one of the many fine sprinting grounds of well maintained track, near Riccall, in 1935. At this period the well known Ivatt Atlantics were still mainly engaged in express main line duties, and it was unusual to find one relegated to a freight train.

One of Gresley's Sandringham class 4-6-0s, built mainly for use on the Great Eastern lines. This one, however, No 2842 *Kilverstone Hall,* together with No 2816 *Fallodon,* spent several years on the Great Central main line, and is seen here in 1934 on a Manchester express near Northwood.

The once busy Great Northern 'Northern Heights' surburban branches to High Barnet, Edgware, and the Alexandra Palace were all scheduled for electrification just before World War II, but this was suspended on the outbreak of hostilities. In the event only the High Barnet branch was completed throughout, and the Edgware branch as far as Mill Hill, both worked as extensions of the London Underground Northern Line, whilst the Alexandra Palace branch was closed and abandoned. This view shows an Alexandra Palace train leaving Highgate Tunnel in 1937 with Gresley N2 0-6-2T No 4741.

A typical scene on the Great North of Scotland during the period. A Manson class P 4-4-0 (LNER D43) No 6812, of 1890, seen leaving Aberdeen on a Deeside train in 1930. Comprised entirely of six-wheelers, some transferred from the Great Eastern. The GNoSR was unique amongst the main line railways of Britain in never having any 0-6-0 tender engines, all of its freight services being worked by the several varieties of 4-4-0, of which this one is fairly representative.

Durham viaduct in 1936. Gresley J39 class 0-6-0 No 1504 passes Pacific No 2561 *Minoru* on an up express.

The Great Eastern had a number of these enclosed tram engines, both 0-4-0s and 0-6-0s, for dockworking and also on the Wisbech and Upwell tramway, one of the last roadside systems of its kind. No 7132 is seen here in 1929 at Outwell on one of the freight trains, which lasted until quite recently, latterly of course with diesel locomotives. The passenger service had already been discontinued as early as January 1928.

One of the Sentinel steam railcars of which the LNER was a wide user during the later 1920s and the 1930s. (The LMS also had a few.) They were painted in an attractive livery of green with cream upper panels, and named after old stage coaches. No 51914 *Royal Forester*, photographed here at Wigan GCR in 1933.

The Great Western Railway

C. B. Collett's *King George V* which, when turned out from Swindon in 1927, with a tractive effort of 40,300 lb was Britain's most powerful passenger locomotive. Later in the year it was shipped to the USA and exhibited at the centenary celebration of the Baltimore & Ohio Railroad, held between 24 September and 15 October 1927. The famous bell which it thereafter carried on its return to England was presented by that company. It still carries it in honourable retirement at Bulmer's cider factory, Hereford, where it is occasionally steamed.

Standing with the charming 'Miss Britannia' is W. A. Stainer, at that time Collett's principal assistant on the GWR at Swindon. In 1932 he was appointed chief mechanical engineer to the LMS, on which railway, as is well known, he revolutionised locomotive design. He later received his knighthood.

Of all the major railways in the British Isles, the Great Western was far ahead of the others in deciding to dispense with four-coupled locomotives for express passenger working. The larger wheeled 6ft 8in varieties, the double framed Badmintons, Atbaras, Flowers, and Cities and even the more modern Churchward outside cylinder Counties fell quickly to the axe, all being taken out of service between 1927 and 1933. The County tank counterpart, 4-4-2Ts, likewise all disappeared between 1931 and 1935.

The smaller wheeled 4-4-0s lasted somewhat longer, some even survived nationalisation, and then there were the hybrid Dukedogs, nominally new engines constructed between 1936 and 1939, but in effect reconstructions with the boilers of the old Duke of Cornwall class on the frames of the later Bulldogs, but none of these were express engines in the true sense.

This view shows a Dean engine No 4109 *Monarch*, built in 1898, at Bath in 1929. It was scrapped in 1931.

Typical GWR view of the 1930s. One of the first of the numerous Hall class, which eventually totalled 330 engines, No 4907 *Broughton Hall*, seen at Lostwithiel in 1935 with a Plymouth-Penzance train.

Branch line scene in 1928. 2-4-0T No 5, one of several built at Swindon in 1869 for working on the Metropolitan lines in London. Seen here on the branch train at Chard, with two milk vans next to the engine. Milk traffic was of great importance on the railways at this period, particularly in the west country. The noisy clang of milk churns on a station platform is now practically a thing of the past.

The Great Western, with its large number of branch lines, was a great user of the 'pull and push' auto train, usually in the hands of one of these Armstrong 0-4-2Ts, with a saloon type trailer, converted from one of the earlier steam rail motors. No 1465 (built 1883) at Yeovil in 1935.

One of Dean's 0-6-0s, No 2368, on a freight train near Brill in 1935. Most of these engines had inside frames, but twenty of them, Nos 2361-2380, built in 1885/6, were turned out as double framers. The overbridge seen in the photograph carried the Metropolitan Brill branch, referred to on page 72.

The early years of the grouping resulted in mass withdrawal of the miscellaneous variety of engines inherited from the South Wales railways. This view, taken at Swindon in 1933, is a typical view of the scrapyard in those years and brings to mind similar views taken 40 years earlier after the abolition of the broad gauge. The South Wales locomotives came in a large variety of shapes and sizes, but a very representative one may be found in the illustration of the Brecon & Merthyr engine on page 33.

The Southern Railway

A LB & SCR surburban scene in pre-electrification days. Stroudley D1 0-4-2T No B218 (originally built in 1885 as No 351 *Chailey*) on a local train from London Bridge at Brockley in 1926, at which time many of these small engines continued to perform extremely efficiently with very heavy loads, considering their size. Most of them ended their days on country branches, often with pull and push trains.

The South Western's No 218 on the Turnchapel branch, Plymouth, in 1924. It duly became SR No E218 and was eventually transferred to the Isle of Wight as No W33 *Bembridge*.

To help out with the busy Kent Coast traffic, at that time entirely in the hands of SE & CR 4-4-0s, some of them ageing South Eastern and London Chatham and Dover engines, the SR transferred ten of Drummond's very efficient T9 class 4-4-0s from the South Western, later increased to fifteen. They performed very efficiently on these services up to World War II. No E304 seen passing Brixton in 1929.

Photographs of freight trains in the Isle of Wight are rare, but this view shows Stroudley E class 0-6-0T No W2 *Yarmouth* (late B152, originally LB & SCR *Hungary*) approaching Newport in 1933, with a coal train from Medina Wharf.

One of Maunsell's ill fated 2-6-4Ts, No A797 *River Mole* on a Brighton Pullman express in 1926. All were withdrawn after the Sevenoaks accident in 1927, and subsequently converted to tender engines.

At the time of the Sevenoaks disaster the remaining unrebuilt F Class Stirling 4-4-0s were about to be withdrawn, but the resulting engine shortage gave them a short reprieve. No A194 is here seen leaving Ashford on a Canterbury train in 1925. Note that a LSWR coach had already been drafted to the SE & CR section, although such transfers had not yet become commonplace as in later years.

One of Wainwright's handsome D class 4-4-0s ascending the one-in-ninety-five out of Bromley South in 1934. Although shorn of its former embellishments, the graceful outline of these engines is still very apparent, and one of them in all its elaborate glory can now be seen in Clapham Museum.

(Opposite above) During the general strike of 1926 the volunteer crews in charge of No A763 named it after the daughter of the then Prime Minister. Although unofficial, it was well executed and remained until the engine's next repaint; this engine can consequently claim to be one of the only two SE & CR built engines ever to carry a name. The other was the original 2-6-4T No 790 of 1917, the name being added in SR days. (The rest of the River class were not built until after the grouping.) This photograph was taken at Hastings old station.

(Below) LSWR Drummond 0-4-4T No E481 at Lymington Pier in 1928. Of particular interest are the pulleys on the cab roof for the early type of pull and push apparatus worked by cables, although obviously not in use on this occasion as the engine was running round its train.

Some of the Brighton Atlantics were transferred to the South Eastern section in the year or so prior to the outbreak of World War II. As with certain other Brighton classes, the cabs had to be modified to suit the more restricted loading gauge. No 2426 *St Albans Head* seen here leaving Bromley on a Ramsgate train in 1938.

The Southern's only steam railcar, built by the Sentinel Co in 1933 (works No 8740). Seen here in that year at The Dyke, which short branch from Brighton into the South Downs was closed entirely on 1 January 1939.

This vehicle was No 6 in a special list of miscellaneous passenger vehicles, Nos 1-4 being the small railbuses and trailers used on the Ryde Pier Tramway, whilst No 5 had been a petrol railcar later sold to the Weston Clevedon & Portishead Railway. No 6 was withdrawn in 1942 and used as an air-raid shelter at Ashford Works for the rest of the war, finally scrapped about 1946.

A very regrettable casualty of 1935 was the closure of the Southern's only narrow-gauge line, the Lynton & Barnstaple. Not only popular with holiday makers, it also served other very useful purposes. One immediate result was a sharp increase in the price of coal in Lynton. With the required imagination and enterprise it could have been kept going, at least for a time, perhaps during the summer months only, but the Southern was not really interested at this period in anything that did not lend itself to electrification. The locomotive stock consisted of five 2-6-2Ts (one built as recently as 1925), and, oddly enough, one American 2-4-2T built by Baldwin in 1900, one of the very few foreign engines ever to work in this country prior to World War II.

The London and South Western engine that never was! One of three acquired by the SR at the grouping from the previously independent Plymouth Devonport & South Western Junction Railway. When it went to Eastleigh for overhaul early in 1923 no decision had yet been made as to the painting of engines under the new regime, so they gave it the old LSWR initials to be going on with. It later received the number 756 in the locomotive list.

Joint Lines

Jointly owned or operated lines, of which the owning partners came into two different groups as a result of the 1923 amalgamation, continued as joint concerns until nationalisation in 1948. So far as outward appearances were concerned, they were in effect usually worked by one, or perhaps both, of the new organisations, but three of them continued to maintain their own individuality. The Cheshire Lines still had its own coaching stock, appropriately lettered CLC, but no locomotives, these being supplied by the LNER and LMS.

Two others, however, still retained their own locomotives and workshops for several years, and remained virtually independent railways outside the scope of the grouping.

The Midland and Great Northern Joint was a long straggling line connecting the Midlands with the east coast through the northern part of East Anglia, chiefly in what was in the main Great Eastern territory.

This view shows a typical M & GN local train meandering over the plains of Lincolnshire near Sutton Bridge in 1936, headed by one of the Beyer Peacock 4-4-0s No 23, built in 1881. The M & GN livery was a distinctive one of yellow, not unlike Stroudley's famous 'improved engine green', but later changed to an equally pleasing darker shade of brown.

One of the very few locomotives actually built at the Melton Constable works of the M & GNR. No 9 was turned out in 1909, and incidentally was one of the last two new engines built for the company, so that by 1937 the average age of the locomotive stock was elderly, to put it mildly. It is seen here at North Walsham in 1929.

Most of the M & GN engines were of pure Midland Railway design, the backbone of the stock consisting of 4-4-0s, corresponding to classes 1 and 2 to be found in the parent system, and 0-6-0s of classes 2 and 3. Except in the case of the class 2 0-6-0s they were not exactly similar in every detail to the corresponding Midland engines, but the variations in the others were slight. Their transfer to the LNER thus made them somewhat incongruous.

Consequently, apart from their age, it is not surprising that most of them got somewhat short shrift when they turned up at Stratford, where they were sent after the closure of the Melton Constable works. Some of them did get an overhaul and repaint, renumbered with the addition of a cypher as LNER 01 etc, but this livery did not settle happily on the Johnson outline, as seen in the picture of No 043 coming off the Cromer branch at Melton Constable in 1939.

Incidentally it is an interesting reflection that when these engines began to turn up at Stratford in early 1938 they were not the first Johnson locomotives to have been seen there, even if for very many years, for he had been loco engineer to the GER prior to his departure for Derby in 1873.

Somerset and Dorset engines also remained separate, with locomotive workshops at Highbridge, until they were absorbed into the LMS stock in 1930. Like the M & GNJ they also had a distinctive livery from the all-too-common greens and blacks, being painted in dark blue.

This view shows two 0-4-0STs, Nos 26A and 45A, built at Highbridge works in 1895, fussily engaged in shunting at Radstock in 1929. There is a small coal deposit in this area and two or three collieries grew up in consequence.

The last passenger engines built for the S & DJR were three standard LMS class 2 4-4-0s, Nos 44-46, turned out from Derby in 1928. This picture shows No 45 at Bath in 1930, just after the absorption of the loco stock by the LMS. Note the new number on the smokebox door in conjunction with the original. This was a very excellent practice which the S & DJR had indulged in on previous renumbered engines, to carry both numbers for a time to enable enginemen to familiarise themselves with the change. When this photograph was taken the engine was still in the S & DJR livery although the initials on the tender had been altered. This temporary appearance was also to be seen on a number of engines at this period, so that the Coronation Pacifics of 1937 were not in fact the only LMS engines to have appeared in this colour, as might have been thought at the time.

S & DJR 0-4-4Ts Nos 14A and 13 at Highbridge in 1928. Exactly why No 14, built in 1877, had to be duplicated by a new 4-4-0 of this number built in 1896, whereas the others remained in the capital stock for the rest of their existence, is one of those oddities for which there is no obvious explanation. Incidentally, both engines Nos 14 and 14A were scrapped in 1930.

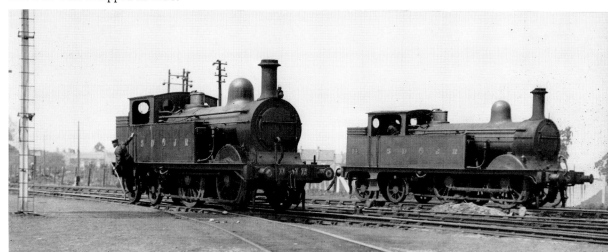

The Metropolitan and Metropolitan District Railways

Metropolitan locomotives were painted in a very attractive dark red, with the name of the company appearing in full on the tank sides. In 1933 one engine, No 105, appeared with the abbreviated MET as illustrated, possibly the only one so to appear before the title was altered to the newly formed London Transport. The red livery was continued, but from 1 November 1937 the steam country working was transferred to the LNER, which absorbed the 'main line' engines into its own stock.

The change-over from electric to steam working at Rickmansworth. This view, taken in 1935, shows electric locomotive No 14, *Benjamin Disraeli*, which had brought the train (behind the photographer) out from Baker Street, running round, with the waiting locomotive, 4-4-4T No 106, already backing out of the engine sidings.

The Brill branch was set in as rural a countryside as could be found anywhere, in complete contrast to the busy London area. This picturesque view, taken in 1935, its last year of operation, shows one of the original Beyer Peacock 4-4-0Ts once used on the Inner Circle in London, No 23, by then under London Transport ownership. It later became LT No L45 and can now be seen, restored to its original condition, in Clapham Museum. Note also the coach with eight rigid wheels, not a bogie vehicle.

(Opposite, above). An early first-class saloon with curved clerestory roof and gated ends, of distinctly American appearance. These vehicles were built about 1905.

Although the Southern and LNER were the principal users of Pullman cars between the wars, the Metropolitan also had a couple, *Mayflower* and *Galatea,* built in 1909. They worked on certain through services to Amersham and Aylesbury. Company directors and other homing business men, after an exhausting day of mergers and other important deals, could relax on their journey from Aldersgate or Moorgate to their comfortable homes in the Chilterns, and fortify themselves with a few drinks into a suitably mellow condition for the evening's entertainment. There was even a late working of one of these cars, leaving Baker Street around midnight, which could be patronised after an evening at the theatre or opera. Such was the enterprise of the old Metropolitan Railway in its efforts to please its customers. This happy state of affairs came to an abrupt end on the outbreak of war, never to be resumed. Business executives, if they do not now travel home in a chauffeur-driven limousine, have to endure the discomfort of a multi-unit train without even the solace of first-class accommodation.

The Metropolitan District Railway retained two of its locomotives for many years after electrification in 1905 for departmental duties. These were Nos 33 and 34, built in 1880. No 33 was scrapped in 1925 and replaced by one of the similar Beyer Peacock type from the Metropolitan Railway, No 22. On transfer it became No 35 (note the legend on the side tank *UndergrounD*). This photograph was taken at Lillie Bridge in 1926. The original District engine was still much in original condition, complete with condensing apparatus. It was finally scrapped in 1932.

Independent and Light Railways

Of the several light and miscellaneous railways not included in the 1921 Railways Act, a list of which will be found in the Grouping Appendix on page 29, of especial interest were those managed by Lieutenant-Colonel H. F. Stephens, already referred to on page 12.

Views of three of these fascinating and colourful lines are given here. Other independent railway illustrations will be found on pages 95 and 101 (Kent & East Sussex), 93 (Mersey), 93 (Liverpool Overhead), and 96 (North Sunderland).

A typical scene on a 'Colonel Stephens' railway. The locomotive yard at Shepherdswell on the East Kent Railway in 1931. In the foreground is No 3, late LSWR 0394, Beattie Ilfracombe goods, built in 1880, already withdrawn from service, but not broken up until the following year. Under repair, on the blocks, is No 4, a Kerr Stuart 0-6-0T of 1917. The remaining engines appear at least to be serviceable, although only one of them is in steam. These are, in order, No 2 *Walton Park*, 0-6-0ST, built by Hudswell Clark in 1908, which had previously worked on both the Weston Clevedon & Portishead and the Shropshire & Montgomeryshire Railway; No 7, another Beattie engine, a 0-6-0ST built in 1882, former LSWR No 0127, No 5, Adams 4-4-2T of 1885, formerly LSWR 0488, and now to be seen on the Bluebell Railway, and No 8, Stirling 0-6-0, late SE & CR No 372.

A similar engine, No 6, late SE & CR No 376, was out working at the time, whilst the only one not already accounted for, No 1, an old Fox Walker 0-6-0ST of 1875, was tucked away in the shed behind the camera.

A somewhat similar scene to that on the previous page, the Chichester & Selsey Railway, or, to give it its full title, Hundred of Manhood & Selsey Tramway (later known as the West Sussex Railway) in 1927. The engines are, 2-4-2T No 1 *Selsey*, built by Peckett & Co in 1897 (works No 681), new for the line. The remainder, all 0-6-0STs were obtained from various sources secondhand: No 5 *Ringing Rock* (Manning Wardle 1883), No 2 *Sidlesham* (Manning Wardle 1861), No 3 *Chichester* (Hudswell Clarke 1903) whilst in the shed is *Morous* No 4 (Manning Wardle 1866), lately transferred from the Shropshire & Montgomeryshire Railway. The railway closed in January 1935.

More miscellanea, this time on the Weston Clevedon & Portishead Railway, a scene in 1929. No 4 *Hesperus*, was built by Sharp Stewart & Co in 1876 for the Watlington & Princes Risborough Railway. This line was absorbed by the GWR in 1883, the engine becoming their No 1384. It was sold in 1911 and acquired by the WC & PR. The condition of the smokebox suggests that it would not have been of any use when the photograph was taken, but it was not cut up until 1937. The 2-4-0T in the rear, No 1 *Clevedon*, was built in 1879 by Messrs Dübs & Co for the Jersey Railway. It was sold by them in 1884 and seems to have worked in Cornwall for a number of years, coming into the hands of the WC & PR in 1906. Although latterly out of use, it was not scrapped until closure of the line in 1940.

A pleasant scene on the beautiful two foot six inch gauge Leek & Manifold Valley Railway in 1933, a year before the line was closed and the trackbed converted to a public footpath. This shows one of the two 2-6-4Ts which were built by Messrs Kitson & Co in 1904, and worked the railway for the whole of its existence. A picture of one of the coaches will be found on page 105. Although a separate company, constructed under the Light Railways Act of 1896, it was worked by the old North Stafford Railway, and consequently came into the hands of the LMS at the grouping, its only narrow-gauge passenger-carrying line.

Another narrow-gauge line, this time two foot three inch gauge, the Campbeltown & Machrihanish, and the most inaccessible railway in the British Isles. The only practicable means of communication was by steamer, a journey of several hours. On the occasion of the author's visit in 1930, the sea passage was very rough, and we were about an hour late arriving at Campbeltown. Without personal inconvenience, I may add, although there were many others not so fortunate. This resulted in the awkward choice of either travelling over the line or visiting the engine shed, some distance away, where I knew there were two or three older locomotives to be seen; there was not time to do both. I am now very thankful that I took what I regard in later years as the right decision, to enjoy the rare experience of 'doing' this most remote of Great Britain's railways. Nowadays Campbeltown can be reached more easily by road. The view shows the train at its outer terminus at Machrihanish, with 0-6-2T *Atlantic*, the company's last engine, built by Andrew Barclay in 1907. The line was closed in 1932, and was Scotland's only narrow-gauge railway, although a number of others were planned during the early 1920s (see page 22).

Irish Railways

The Great Southern & Western was the largest railway in Ireland, and in the natural course of events became the predominating partner in the newly formed Great Southern Railways, created in 1925, whereby all lines wholly within the Republic (then the Free State) became merged into a single entity.

This view shows a typical GSR scene in 1934, on the long-since-closed Achill branch of the Midland Great Western Railway, extending to the western coast. The through train to Dublin is seen taking water at the wayside passing station at Mallaranny, having crossed to the down line to gain access to the water column, and not in any way indicative of right-hand running. Irish railways and roads are of the normal left-hand pattern, as in the rest of the British Isles. Nevertheless, some passing loops, particularly on the NCC, were signalled for bi-directional running, so that the main platform could be used if there was no train to cross, or if one train was non-stop it could be run through the straight road without reduction in speed. The engine in the photograph is a McDonnell 4-4-0 of 1888 in its original condition (many were later superheated) with the unusual type of smokebox door hinged in two sections.

Midland Great Western Railway 0-6-0 No 74 *Luna* in pre-amalgamation livery (later renumbered GSR 576, losing its name). Both the MGWR and the Great Northern named nearly all of their locomotives in former days, including 0-6-0 goods engines, a practice rarely to be found elsewhere. Note also the peculiar design of cab, also a MGWR characteristic. A primitive form of streamlining? Photographed at Broadstone in 1929.

Great Northern Railway. In 1932 this enterprising railway accelerated the timings of its principal expresses between Dublin and Belfast to two hours twenty minutes by the best train (3.15 pm ex Dublin) and two and a half hours by others, for the $112\frac{1}{2}$ miles, the number of intermediate stops varying from three to five.

For this purpose five new 4-4-0 compounds were built, in many ways similar to the famous Deeleys of the MR and LMS. No 86 *Peregrine*, seen here leaving Dublin on the 9.30 am train on 6 June 1932, first day of the new schedules. These fine engines, at first plain black as here depicted, later received the blue livery with red underframes. It may be added that non-stop running was introduced in 1947 with a timing of two and a quarter hours, and the train became known as the Enterprise express.

One of the previously independent railways which came into the Great Southern was the Waterford & Tramore, a $7\frac{1}{4}$ mile line without intermediate stations connecting the city with the seaside resort. It was on the other side of the River Suir from the main system, from which it was entirely isolated without physical connection with any other railway. Like many other Irish lines, its locomotives and rolling stock were ancient to a degree, and one of them was a 2-2-2 WT dating back to 1855. It had the distinction of being the last single wheeler to remain in regular service in the whole of the British Isles and was in constant use until it disgraced itself in 1936 by becoming derailed and falling down an embankment. It was unfortunately cut up on the spot, otherwise it might well have attained its centenary, and what a subject for preservation it would have made! As W & T No 1 it became GSR No 483 and is seen here leaving Tramore in 1932.

The enterprising Midland Railway of England extended its ever widening empire on 1 July 1903 by the acquisition of the Belfast & Northern Counties Railway. It became known as the MR-, and in due course the LMS-NCC, Northern Counties Committee, and over the passage of years the line gradually acquired many of the characteristics of the parent company. It was by the 1930s in many respects a delightful miniature edition of the Midland, not the least in the matter of the well-known crimson lake livery, which was applied to all engines, and all kept in superb condition. The Derby influence was also by this time predominant in the actual design, many of the 4-4-0s in particular showing their unmistakable parentage (some were actually built at Derby), although never quite identical with those to be found on the MR system itself. This 4-4-0 having been built in 1895 is not perhaps quite typical of these changes, although the distinctive Midland chimney will be noted. It was in fact originally one of a pair of two-cylinder Worsdell-von Borries compounds, a type to which the old BNCR had been particularly addicted, built in 1895, although this one, No 50 *Jubilee*, had by this time been rebuilt as a two-cylinder simple. It is seen here in 1930 approaching Larne Harbour with the Stranraer Boat Train.

The LNWR also had an interest over the Irish Sea in the 26½ mile long Dundalk Newry & Greenore Railway. Even more perhaps than in the case of the similarity of the NCC to the Midland just referred to, this line was undeniably pure North Western. The engines, of which there were six, all of the same design as here illustrated, were unmistakably Crewe, even to the number plates, but even here not exactly like anything to be found on the mainland. They were in fact obviously the result of a mating—legitimate or otherwise—between one of the one-time numerous Dx goods introduced by Ramsbottom in 1858 and the Webb 'special tanks', the last survivors of which were to be seen at Wolverton carriage works up to the late 1950s.

The DN & GR was eventually taken over by the Great Northern, and the remaining engines all regrettably cut up in 1952, although there were at the time proposals and strong hopes for the preservation of one of them.

Apart from the normal 5ft 3in, Ireland had a number of light railways constructed to the 3ft 0in gauge, and the Great Southern acquired six such lines at the 1925 amalgamation. This view, on the Schull & Skibbereen, taken at Kilcoe in 1938, may be taken as typical, although naturally all had their own individualities. The engine, No 4, is a 4-4-0T, a type much in favour amongst others on these systems.

Amongst the 3ft 0in gauge lines lying either wholly in Northern Ireland or partly in both countries, thus not coming under the auspices of the Great Southern, was the Londonderry & Lough Swilly, which with the associated Letterkenny & Burtonport Extension, had a main line no less than 74½ miles in length through the wide expanses of County Donegal. This view shows a train from Burtonport pausing to take water at one of the lonely moorland intermediate stations, Gweedore, in 1937. The engine is one of two 4-8-0s, Nos 11 and 12, built by Messrs Hudswell Clarke in 1905. There were also two tank counterparts, 4-8-4Ts Nos 5 and 6, which came out in 1912, and these four engines were unique in that they were the only engines of their respective wheel arrangements, broad or narrow gauge, ever to run in the British Isles.

The Sligo Leitrim & Northern Counties Railway (standard 5ft 3in gauge) was another line which retained its independence owing to the forty-eight mile line being crossed en route by the border between the two countries. At the time of its sudden enforced closure on 1 October 1957, inevitable because of the discontinuance by the Northern Ireland government of the GNR Londonderry line, which at Enniskillen had been the Sligo Leitrim's main outlet with the outside world, it was one of the largest of the few remaining independent railway systems still operating in the British Isles.

Its small stud of locomotives was unique in that they were distinguished by names only, never having received numbers, a custom for the like of which, on a main public railway, one must go back to the days of the broad-gauge single-wheelers on the Great Western in the nineteenth century. Latterly the locomotive stock had consisted of ten 0-6-4Ts, two of quite recent construction (being in fact the last new steam engines built for any Irish railway), but five of them of much older design dating back to 1882-1899, were of outstanding archaic appearance, as shown by this picture of *Lissadell* taken at Sligo in 1929.

On the outskirts of Dublin there ran until 1933 one of the last examples of a road-side steam tramway to be found in the British Isles, the Dublin & Blessington. This view, taken from the upper deck of one of the cars in 1932, shows a double-ended 2-4-2T, with a cab both fore and aft, No 10, the last acquisition by the company, built by Messrs T. Green of Leeds in 1906.

The Giant's Causeway Portrush & Bush Valley Tramway, of 3ft gauge in Northern Ireland, has a justifiable claim to the distinction of Britain's first electric railway, although it was forestalled in actual electric operation by a few weeks by Volk's small line on the front at Brighton. Some of the original cars are seen here at Giant's Causeway in 1930.

Train Services

A typical Great Eastern suburban train in the 1930s on the intensive 'jazz' service first introduced in 1922. Holden 2-4-2T No 7578 on a train for Gidea Park.

The up Atlantic Coast Express about to enter Honiton Tunnel, August Bank Holiday 1928. The train, which on this busy day ran in two or perhaps three parts, comprised coaches from various terminals such as Plymouth, Padstow, Bude, and Ilfracombe, from any of which the main rump of the train may have originated (the pattern varied over the years), and each being coupled up at the appropriate junctions. The engine is King Arthur No 746 *Pendragon*, one of the original Urie series of 1922, and the fifth vehicle is a clerestory dining car, one of the very few of that type owned by the LSWR.

A pleasing sight of former days now gone for ever. The branch 'local' quietly simmering in its bay platform awaiting the arrival of the main connecting train before pursuing its leisurely way to its destination. Nowadays such a facility would normally be provided by an omnibus, or in the few cases where rail connection still survives, by a diesel railcar.

This particular scene was pictured at Dingwall on the Highland Railway in 1928, and the actual occasion is referred to in some detail on page 18. The southbound train referred to in that little account had already departed, and the Fortrose train, with 'Skye Bogie' No 14277, was still awaiting the connection from the south, now standing at the platform headed by No 14420 *Ben a 'Chait* and 14404 *Ben Clebrig,* bound for Wick.

Somerset & Dorset Joint Railway. The Pines Express through train between the North West, Midlands, and Bournemouth, seen here at Templecombe in 1936. The lines on the left led up to the SR station, where the train called, afterwards reversing to the point beyond the signals before it could continue its journey southwards, as seen in the picture. A pilot engine would be attached at the rear to perform this operation.

The engines are standard LMS class 2 4-4-0s Nos 631 and 635, the latter actually being a genuine Somerset & Dorset loco, built at Derby in 1928, one of three of a batch which was under construction for the LMS itself at the time, but which were appropriated by the S & D, which was short of motive power. On the absorption of Somerset & Dorset engines into LMS stock, in 1930, these three S & DJR Nos 44-46 became Nos 633-635, following No 632, which number had by then been reached on the parent system.

Before tram and omnibus competition made such trains unremunerative, and perhaps superfluous, there were a great many through local services giving easy inter-communication with the outskirts of London, particularly between the north and south, by means of such important links as the Farringdon-Ludgate Hill connection from the Metropolitan 'widened' lines to the SE & CR, and Chelsea bridge on the West London Extension Railway. Most of these services had disappeared before World War I, but an interesting survival into the late 1920s was a daily through train between Willesden, on the LMS, over the West London line and East Croydon via the Crystal Palace, on the SR.

Its main function was to carry parcels traffic, but it was still available for any passengers who might wish to avail themselves of its facilities, as late as 1928, when this photograph was taken of it entering Clapham Junction en route for Willesden.

It will be noted that the engine, LNWR 2-4-2T No 2510, is still in its pregrouping state, although five years after the amalgamation. As already mentioned, Crewe was very reluctant to fall in with the renumbering scheme or to accept the Derby decree of Midland red livery, to which this engine would have been entitled during the early years. As it was, it escaped this indignity and when it did finally become LMS 6534, it was in plain black, more in accordance with LNWR ideas. Note the coincidence of the number 2510, as in this illustration and opposite (lower).

(Opposite, above). That vital link between north and south, the West London Extension, also saw many through main-line services between the north of England and the south coast resorts. Here, in August 1933, a through train of a very mixed rake of coaches from Liverpool and Manchester calls at Kensington en route to the southeast, conveying holidaymakers from the industrial north to Herne Bay, Margate and Ramsgate, etc. The SR engine, a SE & CR rebuilt D1 class 4-4-0 No 1743, had replaced the LMS one at Willesden Junction. Addison Road, which at that time even boasted a refreshment room, is now shorn of its former glory, although it has come into its own again to a small extent as a useful station for motorail services and the like. The local trains have, however, all but disappeared, curtailed to a couple of morning and evening trains to Clapham Junction, and a shuttle service from Earls Court when there is an exhibition at Olympia. The regular electric trains to Willesden and to the Metropolitan lines disappeared during World War II and have never been restored.

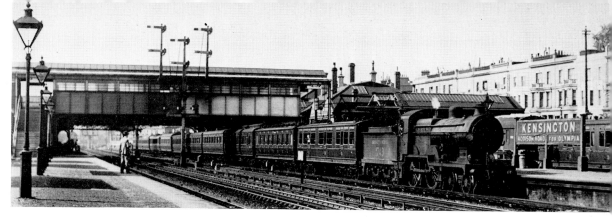

Britain's first streamlined express, the Silver Jubilee, introduced by Sir Nigel Gresley, seen here leaving Newcastle on 14 May 1936 on its 268½ miles non-stop run to King's Cross in 240 minutes. The startling change in aesthetic standards from the hitherto conventional outline of a locomotive, was the subject of much criticism, both favourable and unfavourable. From a dynamic point of view streamlining of a locomotive and train was found to be of appreciable advantage at speeds of 90 mph or more, which of course was necessary with this new schedule, but apart from this the 'new look' had an undoubted publicity value with the general public, if not with the railway enthusiasts of the time.

Another departure from long established custom was the chime (seen in the unusual position of in front of the chimney) in place of the old established engine whistle, compared with which the somewhat jazzy sound of the new creation seemed perhaps to reflect the changing fashions of the age. The more dulcet and symphonic tones of the steam era are heard no more on our main lines, but one recollects that even these varied greatly amongst the different railways, from the very high-pitched note of the Great North of Scotland to the distinctive hooters of the Caledonian (later adopted by Stanier on the London Midland & Scottish). Between these two extremes, amongst the most melodious were the whistles of the Lancashire & Yorkshire, Great Central, Midland, and Great Western Railways. Great Northerns were somewhat on the shrill side, and it may not now be very well remembered that the small Isle of Wight Railway had again very high-pitched whistles which could be heard alongside the deep hooters of the Isle of Wight Central.

But how pleasant all of them were in comparison with the strident blaring horns in the diesel and electric age of today.

The LMS in due course followed suit by the inauguration on 5 July 1937 of the Coronation Scot, which reduced the time between Euston and Glasgow to 6½ hours, concurrently with a corresponding train, the Coronation on the LNER, King's Cross to Edinburgh in six hours.

The engine masquerading as No 6229 *Duchess of Hamilton*, seen here passing Berkhamsted on 11 July 1939, shortly prior to the outbreak of World War II, was in fact the original 6220 *Coronation*, which had exchanged names and numbers with the real 6229, then on tour in the United States. On the latter's return to this country, delayed owing to war conditions until 1940, the two engines resumed their original identities, perhaps a great mistake, as many American servicemen by now in this country, seeing the real 6220, were naturally under the erroneous impression that it was the same locomotive which had toured their own native land.

The newly inaugurated through Paris-London ferry train passing Bromley on 18 October 1936 during its first week of operation. The engines were Maunsell 4-4-0 L1 class No 1758 with Wainwright L class No 1764. Sometimes the train would be hauled by a Lord Nelson 4-6-0, but it tended to be too heavy for a single engine with anything up to a dozen of the weighty 'Wagons Lits' sleeping cars plus vans, and it was found it could be better handled with a couple of modern superheated 4-4-0s.

Electrification

An early train on the first section of the SE & CR to be electrified, the service from Victoria and Holborn Viaduct to Orpington. Seen at Petts Wood, on the down burrowing junction from the former LC & DR line (out of sight behind the trees) to the SER main line (bottom left) from Charing Cross. The early composition of these trains, as on the original LSWR system, was of three-coach units, worked singly in the slack hours or in pairs at the busy times, and supplemented at peak periods by two non-powered trailers sandwiched between the two sets. The reforming of the train, however, proved something of a nuisance, and eventually this method of operation was abandoned, the permanent electric units being strengthened to four coaches. The snake-like appearance of these trains coupled with the green livery gave rise to the nickname of 'caterpillars'.

The LB & SCR had pioneered electrification on what was later to become the Southern Railway as long ago as 1909, when the line between Victoria and London Bridge was converted, with 6,600 volt alternating current and overhead wires. This was later extended to the Crystal Palace in 1912, finally to Coulsdon and Sutton in 1925.

An up Crystal Palace train is seen here passing Wandsworth Common on 17 March 1928.

The trains for the last overhead electric extension, mentioned above, were composed of separate electric locomotives, sandwiched between two pairs of trailing coaches, with drivers' compartments at the outer ends. This system was short lived, however, as in the intrests of standardisation it was decided to convert all of the LB & SC electrified area to the LSWR system of 600 volt direct current with third-rail pick-up, and this was done in 1929. In many ways an unfortunate decision, as the overhead system would have been far more suitable to the eventual main-line electrification which now covers the greater part of the SR network, but this was hardly envisaged at the time.

(Above) A scene on the Liverpool Overhead Railway in 1932, train entering Pier Head station. This was Britain's only elevated railway, and although it was a busy line running through dockland which served a useful purpose in relieving road congestion it was nevertheless closed at the end of 1956 and dismantled.

(right) One of the original coaches built by the LNWR in 1916 for the Watford and Richmond electrification, with Oerlikon equipment. This particular saloon trailer was originally LNWR No 324E. It was withdrawn in 1960.

(bottom right) Mersey Railway, first-class saloon trailer No 60, built in 1902. Seen here at Birkenhead Park. It became 28796 in the LMS series and was withdrawn in 1956 under BR.

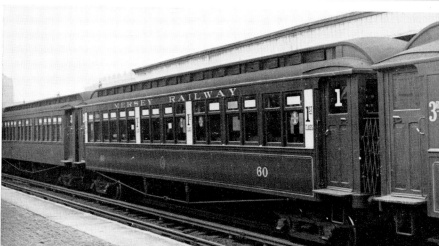

93

Train on the Midland Railway's experimental electrified line between Lancaster and Morecambe and Heysham. The nearer trailer No 2240 was built in 1907 and withdrawn in 1952 as LMS 29291.

Glasgow's only underground line, the Subway, was still cable operated when this photograph was taken at Partick Cross in 1930. In 1935 it was converted to electric traction. Although similar in general appearance to earlier tube stock to be found on London's Underground, the coaches are much smaller and trains consist only of two or three cars. The gauge is four feet.

Internal Combustion

Although there had been some early experiments at the beginning of the century with the application of the petrol engine for railway purposes, it was not until the period between the wars and the development of the diesel that its real possibilities began to be explored.

Lieutenant-Colonel Stephens was one of the first engineers to investigate the practicality of reducing running expenses by introducing what were in effect omnibuses adapted for rail traction. The unit consisted of two buses, coupled back to back, sometimes with an open wagon in between them. Only the engines in the leading car would be engaged, the other being trailed backwards out of gear. The first of these units, which had Ford engines, appeared in 1923 on the Shropshire & Montgomeryshire, and a second one was obtained with Wolseley-Siddeley engines. Later, similar vehicles were in use on the Selsey and the Kent & East Sussex, and also on the Derwent Valley Light Railway (not one of Colonel Stephens' lines). Still further examples, this time with Shefflex engines, appeared on the Selsey and the K & ESR, as shown in this photograph taken at Rolvenden in 1931. It may be added that these contraptions were exceedingly noisy and uncomfortable to ride in.

One of the very first diesel shunters was this ninety-horsepower machine built in 1929 by Messrs Kerr Stuart & Co for the Eskdale Railway in Cumberland. This is well known as a miniature fifteen inch gauge tourist line, but at that period it also operated $2\frac{1}{2}$ miles of standard gauge track serving a stone quarry. This was abandoned in 1953, when the engine was sold to the National Coal Board for use at Wingate Colliery, Durham. It was sold a second time in 1968 to a firm at Lichfield, and is believed to be still in existence and with a possibility of preservation.

Another light railway to explore the possibility of diesel traction at an early date was the 4 mile North Sunderland. *The Lady Armstrong*, seen here at Seahouses in June 1934, was built by Messrs Armstrong Whitworth & Co in 1933 (works No D25).

The first diesel shunter on a main line was this LMS conversion of 1931, which had a Paxman engine with hydrostatic transmission. It was actually built on the frames of a Johnson 0-6-0T No 1831, which number and identity it assumed, so that it can properly be regarded as a rebuild, albeit a somewhat drastic one. It is very obviously the pioneer of the well-known standard diesel shunter of today.

Another early and not very well known diesel shunter was built in 1933 by John Fowler & Co, Leeds (works No 19451) and sold to the Great Western Railway, becoming their No 1 in the locomotive stock. It was disposed of in 1940.

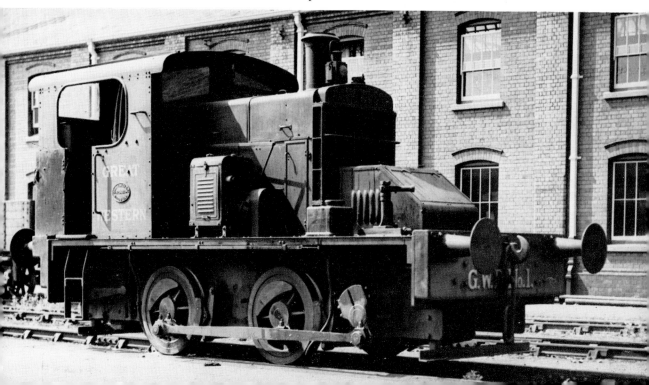

To the three-foot-gauge County Donegal Railway in Ireland falls the distinction of introducing the first diesel railcar in the British Isles. This was No 7 in their fleet of internal combustion vehicles (they already had some petrol railbuses, one of which dated back to 1906). It had a Gardner 74 hp engine, and seated thirty-two passengers. It was hardly the acme of comfort, but later developments had the passenger accommodation embodied in a separate unit, articulated with the power bogie, which was a considerable improvement. Seen here at Strabane with a trailer, converted from a small petrol railcar originally belonging to the Castlederg and Victoria Bridge Railway.

The Great Western was the first main-line railway to introduce diesel railcars, which it did on a not inconsiderable scale from 1934 onwards, eighteen being in service by the commencement of World War II. They were single units of streamlined design. Some of them were intended for long distance operation, and had lavatory facilities, and three of them even small buffets. This view taken in 1938, shows No 9 on the main line near Frome. This particular one was destroyed by fire in 1945.

In 1932 this Michelin railcar with pneumatic-tyred wheels was sent over from France for trials, and made a few trips between Bletchley and Oxford. One noticeable characteristic was its absolute silence from the track or lineside, even to the point of being dangerous, as one had no audible warning of its approach. It never ran in public service.

The last railcar development before such experiments were halted by World War II was by the LMS, who built this streamlined unit at Derby in 1938. The three cars were numbered 80000-80002. Accommodation was for 24 first-class passengers, and 138 third-class. It weighed 73 tons as against a comparable locomotive and coaches of about 173 tons. It was tried out between Oxford and Cambridge and later on the main line between St Pancras and Nottingham.

It was not used during the war, and was withdrawn in 1945.

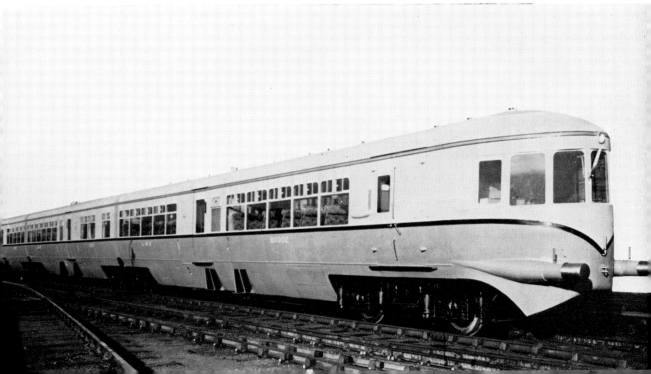

Coaching Stock

Four-wheeled coaches were becoming rare on the main-line railways by 1927, when this photograph was taken at Fort William, showing the Banavie Pier branch train in charge of NBR No 9298 *Glen Shiel*, with GNR 2-6-0 No 4697 backing out after having worked the main-line train from Glasgow. The lower slopes of Ben Nevis can be seen in the background. These two old North British coaches, Nos 3168 and 31087, were, however, still performing a useful function on this long since abandoned short branch which gave connection with the paddle steamer *Gondolier* on its journey up the Caledonian Canal to Inverness, another service which is now no more. The leisurely progress on the open deck, in spite of its wonderful scenic attractions, would hold too little appeal against the modern rush for speed in enclosed motor coaches or private cars

Great Western four-wheeler No 177 still in use on a workmen's train on the Longbridge-Halesowen line in 1935. The engine is one of the numerous pannier tanks to be found all over the system, No 1524, built at Wolverhampton in 1879 and withdrawn in 1939.

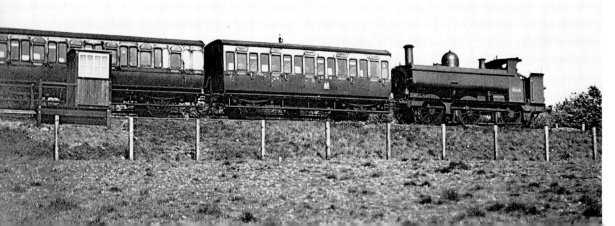

An interesting survival to be found on the Kent & East Sussex Railway in the 1930s. It was purchased in 1905 as an inspection saloon for Lieutenant-Colonel Stephens, and had been built in 1848 as a royal coach for the LSWR, but to what use it was put in later days by that railway is lost in obscurity. It was sometimes employed on ordinary passenger use on the K & ESR as it was often the only serviceable vehicle on the line with lighting. It was sold to the SR in 1936, but its eventual fate seems to be unknown.

LBSC six-wheeled saloon in use in 1926 at Bognor as the shed foreman's office. Mr Powell, the foreman, standing alongside.

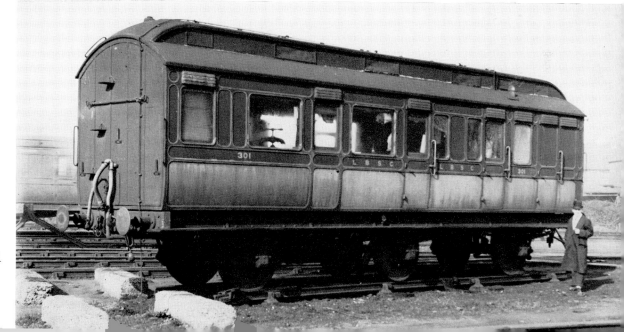

Three interesting coaching stock views taken at the same location at Bromley, Southern Railway (in fact the windows of the author's residence at the time) and all of them away from their owning companies' systems. A beautiful LNWR twelve-wheeled dining car of 1901. Originally 258, later 5258, it became LMS 10463 and finally 263. Withdrawn 1934. Photographed 6 August 1932 on one of the through trains between the north and south-east mentioned on page 88.

LNER open 52 foot 6 inch saloon built at York in 1936 for the GER section, photographed on 21 June in that year when brand new, although how it came to appear on the SE section of the SR is somewhat of a mystery.

GWR corridor third No 5218, built 1929, photographed on 27 August 1933.

Another view at the same spot, this time of a SR train. The engine, No 1312, a SE & CR Wainwright H class tank of 1906, photographed on 2 April 1934, with a train of six-wheelers. These old coaches were normally kept in reserve and only brought out at holiday times (this was Easter weekend) being used on commuter trains, much to the disgust of the season-ticket holders, the regular sets being diverted to holiday relief traffic.

Part of an LNER tri-composite set for the GNR suburban lines with an Edgware train at Mill Hill in 1937. The view shows 43ft brake third No 46421, and part of 34ft 3inch first/second compo No 46422. Second class lasted on the GNR and GER suburban services until 31 December 1937. The GNR and LNER made considerable use of articulated sets, not only for surburban trains, but also introduced by Gresley in 1921 to mainline working with a quintuple restaurant car train for the London-Leeds service.

Great Eastern corridor first with recessed doors. 48 ft 3 in. Built in 1903 as GER 287 for the Harwich boat trains. Seen here as LNER 6407 at Stratford in 1937. Withdrawn from service 1941.

LSWR 'gated' saloon, built at Eastleigh in 1914, on a rail motor train at Guildford in 1933. This vehicle was in service until 1956.

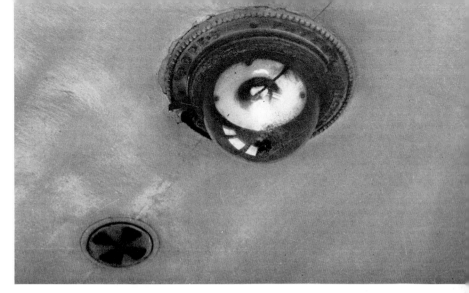

A memory of gas lighting on the old GNR, which persisted on some secondary lines, such as the service between Grantham, Nottingham, Derby, and Stafford, until after World War II. On these particular vehicles some rain always seemed to seep from the roof and accumulated in the glass bowl, and I remember as a very small boy watching with fascination this dirty accumulation with its inevitable dead flies, soot, and what not, as it slopped about with the motion of the train in these none-too-well riding six-wheelers. The piece of apparatus on the left is of course a ventilator for the use of the occupants of the compartment when the ensuing fug under winter conditions got too unbearable, short of the primitive method of opening the window with its accompanying draughts, and was perhaps a very early form of air conditioning.

Two of the four coaches built in 1903 by the Electric Railway & Tramway Carriage Works for the two-foot-six-inch gauge Leek & Manifold Valley Light Railway. Of distinctly foreign appearance, with their end verandahs and extended roofs, these served the needs of the railway until its closure in 1935, when they were withdrawn and subsequently burnt. The nearest vehicle is third saloon No 14991, and the second one a brake compo No 14989.

Shipping, Road and Air

Many of the railways possessed their own steamers, particulary the constituents of the Southern in connection with their cross-channel workings, the LMS for their services to Ireland and the Isle of Man, the Great Western to the Channel Islands, and also to Southern Ireland, and the LNER again to the Continent, including Scandinavia. Many of these were of course, of small liner proportions with full cabin accommodation. This interesting view, however, shows a small twin screw steamer of only 117 tons, owned by the Great Western Railway, *The Mew*, which used to be well known to holidaymakers at Kingswear, where it operated the short ferry crossing to Dartmouth, across the estuary of the Dart. It was built in 1908 by Messrs Cox & Co of Falmouth. During World War II it took part in the Dunkirk evacuation.

The Harwich-Zeebrugge ferry boat, inaugurated on 24 April 1924.

A railway owned omnibus photographed on 14 May 1928.

Experimental Karrier ro-railer, designed for running on either rail or road, seen here on trial on the Harpenden-Hemel Hempstead branch in 1931. As is fairly self-evident in the illustration, the change-over was operated by a arrangement of locking gear, which operation took about five minutes, and was carried out on a suitably designed ramp. It was put into service on the old Stratford on Avon & Midland Junction Railway to convey passengers from Stratford to the Welcombe Hotel, but does not appear to have been much of a success, as it quietly faded away.

The railways' interests during the 1930s were operated by an organisation known as Railway Air Services Limited, with headquarters at Airway Terminus, Victoria Station, London SW1. It was formed jointly by the four group railways and Imperial Airways, and incorporated on 21 March 1934. During 1936 Coast Lines Limited obtained a share of holiday interest and representation on the board. The routes operated varied from year to year, but may be summarised as follows:

On behalf of the LMS: London-Birmingham, -Stoke, -Manchester, -Liverpool, -Belfast, -Glasgow, also to the Isle of Man

GWR 1935 Liverpool, Birmingham, Cardiff. 1937 Bristol, Weston, Cardiff, Torquay, Plymouth.

GWR & SR Joint 1936 Nottingham, Birmingham, Bristol, Southampton, Portsmouth, Shoreham. 1937 extended to serve Liverpool.

Services were also flown by Spartan Airways to the Isle of Wight, and by Channel Island Airways to Jersey and Guernsey. The fleet in 1937 consisted of three DH86 four-engine aircraft with ten seats, eight DH89 twin-engine, ten seats, and three DH84 twin-engine with eight seats, but by 1939 this had been reduced to three DH86 and one DH89.

This view shows one of these machines at Neptune West Tower at the now closed Croydon Airport.

108

Stations

Carlisle in pre-grouping days. The date is uncertain, but it could not have been earlier than 1915, the year in which the Glasgow & South Western 4-4-0 No 327, seen on the left, was built. The absence of any evidence of military personnel proceeding on or returning from leave seems to indicate that it belongs to the period at least not before 1920, and can be said to be representative of that period. It shows a typical crowd of passengers of the

time awaiting the arrival of a southbound express, or perhaps some of them were destined for Newcastle on a North Eastern train which would use the bay platform on the right. A down Midland express has obviously only just arrived, as the 4-4-0 compound has not yet been taken off the train, to be replaced by either a G & SWR or NBR loco, according to destination Glasgow or Edinburgh. A LNWR Claughton awaits on the centre road, possibly to take over from a Caledonian engine on a London express. Carlisle was indeed a fascinating station in those days.

Derby Midland station in 1924. with tram and typical road vehicles of the period. Although the train shed and interior has been modernised of recent years, the old exterior façade still stands practically unaltered today.

Paddington station in the early 1930s when the railways were campaigning for more equitable opportunities of meeting the growing challenge of road competition.

Leyburn station, on the now closed Northallerton-Hawes branch of the North Eastern Railway on 29 June 1927, the occasion of the total eclipse of the sun, an event which will not again be seen in this country until 11 August 1999. It was visible in its entirety only over a narrow belt of country, extending from west to east through Lancashire and Yorkshire, and overnight excursions were run from many parts to view this unforgettable spectacle. Returning passengers are here seen awaiting their trains. This normally quiet small country town station had probably very rarely seen crowds of this sort, and very likely never did again.

Since 1919 the construction of entirely new fully manned stations, that is, apart from halts about to be mentioned, was on a very limited scale. Most of it occurred on the Southern Railway on its gradually expanding electrification in the outer London area where new housing estates and community centres began to sprout with amazing rapidity. Typical of these was Petts Wood, near Orpington, opened on 9 July 1928, and this picture, taken on 14 May 1932, shows an up Continental express passing through, headed by King Arthur No 770 *Sir Prianius*. As can be seen, the new station was at that time situated in open countryside, all very soon to be quickly built over, and now virtually a small township of its own. The Southern had the foresight to provide the travelling facilities before they were actually needed, a policy which in the long run certainly paid off. Almost too much so, in fact it may almost be said to have back-fired, for, as is well known, the SR and BR have for many years found themselves with more traffic than they can comfortably handle in the busy periods.

Another new station intended mainly for commuters and local workers at a large paper mill nearby was opened on 22 September 1938, this time at Apsley on the old LNWR main line, the inaugural train being hauled by 2-6-4T No 2446. It broke the rather long section between Kings Langley and Boxmoor, and the train service was not merely adequate, but very good during the rush hours, being probably the most convenient and comfortable—never overcrowded—of any commuter service out of London.

Amongst the four groups, the Great Western in particular attempted to meet the growing threat of omnibus competition during the 1930s by the construction of a large number of unstaffed halts, both on main lines and branches, to give nearer access to townships and villages, the distance of which from the station often put them at a serious disadvantage compared with road transport. The GWR, moreover, were the largest users of motor trains, which could conveniently call at such points, the guard being responsible for the issue and collection of tickets, a practice which has grown considerably in recent years, where such rural services still exist, although very few actual branches as such still remain. Goonhavern, on the now closed Newquay-Chacewater branch, in Cornwall, was typical of such halts, many of which had the pagoda-like roof on the small corrugated iron shelter.

Not a great deal of major rebuilding of large stations took place between the wars, Waterloo perhaps being the most important undertaking, completed in 1922 after being delayed by the war. Swansea, on the GWR, received a considerable uplift, as seen in this picture taken on 10 August 1926. The 'Bulldog' 4-4-0 cannot unfortunately be identified.

Wimbledon, on the old LSWR, presented a very different appearance from today on 19 February 1928, when this photograph was taken during its reconstruction. The view is looking in a southerly direction, the platform in the foreground being for the then unelectrified services to Ludgate Hill and West Croydon. Note the old-fashioned cast-iron 'Gents', rarely to be found in these more sophisticated days, except perhaps occasionally run across at some wayside country station where such still exist.

Another important reconstruction of the Southern Railway occurred at Epsom, as depicted in this photograph taken on 10 February 1929.

In pregrouping days the LSWR and LB & SCR each had its own station, but the line between Epsom and Leatherhead was jointly owned by both companies. The old Epsom LSWR station consisted of four roads, the two centre ones, without platforms, being used by the LB & SCR trains. After the grouping this arrangement was obviously unsatisfactory, and the station was therefore completely rebuilt so that the trains of both former companies could be accommodated, and the old LB & SCR Epsom Town closed.

This view, looking north, shows the former Brighton lines diverging to the right, with the South Western towards Ewell, of which only the down road was in situ at this particular moment, on the left.

New Construction

A new single-line loop between the Aylesbury and High Wycombe lines at Neasden. with running in one direction only, was built in 1923, in preparation for the Wembley Exhibition held in 1924/5. Until 1968 it was in regular use by special trains in connection with football matches and other events held at Wembley Stadium.

The engine working one of the regular service of one-way trains running from Marylebone back to Marylebone without reversal is a newly constructed GER N7 0-6-2T No 997 E, several of which were on loan to Neasden shed for the extra traffic. On the right can be seen the experimental never-stop railway running through the Exhibition grounds (see below). The building directly ahead was the Indian Pavilion, whilst in the foreground is the reconstructed miniature replica of Old London Bridge.

The never-stop railway. The cars were propelled by a rotary spiral in a well between the tracks. The spiral widened out to give a speed of some ten or twelve mph between stations where it narrowed so as to provide a very low rate of about one or two mph, at which passengers could join or alight with safety. The cars also closed together through the stations; on the in-between stretches they separated by several yards. A semi-circular loop was provided at each terminal, thus the service literally never stopped during its hours of operation.

114

Scene at Torrington on 27 July 1925, the opening day of the newly constructed railway to Halwill Junction, the last standard gauge rural branch line to be built in this country. It was at first worked by these Adams 4-4-0s, later superseded by E1R Brighton 0-6-2Ts, and finally in its last years by LMS type 2-6-2Ts (it remained steam worked almost until the end). This photograph, of indifferent quality owing to the conditions under which it was taken, is included on account of its historical interest. This was one of those appallingly wet days which the West Country can produce when it has a mind, even in midsummer. It will be noted that it was a mixed train consisting of one passenger coach and a tail of wagons.

Ramsgate Harbour, closed by the SR in 1926. The awkward tunnel approach was later reopened as a privately owned two-foot narrow-gauge electric railway, which provided a useful connecting link with the seashore from the SR at its newly built Dumpton Park station during the summer months, until it ceased operation in 1965.

In Northern Ireland, an important cut-off was brought into use in 1934 which avoided reversal of trains between Belfast and Portrush or Londonderry at Greenisland, saving as much as twenty minutes on the journey. It involved the construction of a large new reinforced concrete viaduct, as seen in the illustration.

Again in Northern Ireland, a new bridge was built at Londonderry over the River Foyle in 1933, a double deck affair, the lower of which provided through rail communication between the four railways serving the city, two broad and two narrow gauge, one of each on either side of the river, which had never previously had physical interconnection. It was by its nature only suitable for the transfer of vans and wagons, effected by means of capstans. So far as is known it was never traversed by locomotives. Apart from weight considerations, the turntables could not have accommodated a wheelbase of more than about eighteen feet.

The period between the wars saw the beginnings of the gradual replacement by upper quadrant signals of the usual lower semaphores and the distinctive 'somersaults' of the Great Northern. (The Great Western alone, with its usual independence, remained faithful to its own type of lower quadrants.) This view shows Derby North Junction in 1932, an early gantry of the new type.

Colour-light signalling began to appear in the 1930s, at first in the form of a single-aspect yellow replacing distant signals. The picture on the left, taken in 1935, shows what is believed to be the first intermediate block stop signal on the LMS, between Welton and Weedon, which replaced Buckby Bank box. The second aspect was provided in case of failure of the main light, a Ministry of Transport requirement.

The right-hand view is at Willesden Junction, new line. The two lower aspects are for the bay platforms.

Brentwood Bank in 1939; it will be noted that colour-light signalling had by this time made its appearance in the old Great Eastern London suburban area, although only on certain sections. The engines are No 2870 *City of London*, one of the two Sandringham class given streamlined casing for working the East Anglian express. The other is a rebuilt **B12** 4-6-0 No 8540.

Accidents

A very brief reference to accidents between the wars, as this subject has been very fully covered by two recent books devoted entirely to it, the most recent by the publishers' own *Railway Accidents of Great Britain and Europe*.

On the whole, the railways had a remarkably clean record of accidents during this period. A total of seventeen which come under the category of major disasters over a period of twenty-one years cannot be called catastrophic by any standards, compared with the present-day carnage on the roads, or the results of a single major air disaster, although any one railway accident taken in isolation is liable to present a distorted picture. To mention only a few, there was, for instance, Abermule on the Cambrian on 16 January 1921, a head-on collision on a single line; Owencarrow on the Letterkenny & Burtonport Extension Railway, in Donegal, when the train was blown off a viaduct in a gale; Sevenoaks on 24 August 1927, referred to elsewhere in this book; and Charfield, 13 October 1928, when the results of the double collision were magnified by a disastrous fire, by no means the first time on the old Midland, where gas lighting was still widely used on the wooden coaches, and which certainly accelerated its replacement by electricity.

The Great Western had a very clean record during this period; it must be remembered to its credit that this railway was the first to adopt automatic train control, giving an audible warning to the driver of a signal at danger.

Most of these major accidents have already been illustrated elsewhere, but this view shows what might perhaps be classed as a minor incident, albeit that four passengers were killed. This occurred at Swanley Junction, on the old SE & CR, on Sunday evening 27 June 1937, when the 9.30 am Ashford to Victoria train up the Maidstone East line overran signals, the line being set for an approaching train from the Chatham line in conjunction with a points diversion from the Maidstone direction into a siding into which the express travelled at speed. This, taken on the following day, illustrates the results, but exactly what object could be attained by sheeting over the L class engine No 1768, it is difficult to understand.

Centenaries

LNER *Flying Scotsman* in the Palace of Engineering at Wembley Exhibition in 1925. It will be noted that it has here a six wheeled tender borrowed from a K3 class 2-6-0. Other engines on exhibition were No 200 of the last mentioned class, LMS 4-6-4T No 11114, GWR *Pendennis Castle* and *North Star* replica, SR 2-6-0 No A866, LNWR *Columbine* and Furness *Coppernob*.

The exhibition at Darlington in 1925 in connection with the centenary celebrations. In the foreground are Canterbury & Whitstable *Invicta*, Great Southern & Western Railway Bury 2-2-2 No 36, behind which are two Belgian exhibits and many others.

The LMS 1930 Centenary Exhibition at Wavertree Park, Liverpool showing the *Rocket* (replica) and *North Star* (replica), LNWR *Columbine* and *Cornwall*, MR Johnson 4-2-2 No 118, and other locos.

Lion on view at Euston in September 1938 on the occasion of the centenary of the London & Birmingham Railway.

Preservation

LB & SCR Stroudley 0-4-2 *Gladstone*, restored to original condition through the efforts of the Stephenson Locomotive Society, the first example in this country of a privately preserved project. Seen here at Clapham Junction on 24 May 1927 en route from Battersea Park to York, where the LNER accommodated it in their museum and where it is still to be seen.

Highland Jones goods No 103, built by Sharp Stewart in 1894, the first 4-6-0 in the British Isles. Seen here in 1938 in St Rollox works as first restored by the LMS, in HR green and before replacement of the smokebox wing plates. These were fitted on the engine during resuscitation to working order by BR, when it also received its present yellow livery. After working for several years as enthusiasts' specials during the 1960s, together with the Caledonian single, seen on the right, both engines are now permanently installed in Glasgow Transport Museum.

Another private preservation scheme, this time by the Railway Correspondence & Travel Society, but unfortunately on this occasion abortive, was the Isle of Wight 2-4-0T *Ryde*, built in 1864. Seen here in Eastleigh paint shop in 1936, already partly restored in shop grey, unfortunately sufficient funds were not forthcoming by the outbreak of war, and very regrettably it succumbed to the scrap drive. The engine in the rear is Dugald Drummond's famous 4-2-4T combined engine and inspection saloon, which was also laid aside, but whether with any thoughts of preservation is not certain. Anyway, if there was any such idea it came to nothing, and the engine was scrapped in August 1940.

As mentioned on page 26 the LMS started a small collection at Derby in 1929, which included four Midland engines, and which were all repainted in old MR style for preservation. Kirtley 0-6-0 No 421, a veteran of 1856, is shown below. It had worked until 1926, latterly under the numbers 2320 and 2385. The last Johnson single, No 673, withdrawn in 1928, was similarly laid aside and repainted as MR 118 in 1929, to be followed in 1930 by Kirtley 2-4-0 No 1, given its old number 156A, and Johnson 0-4-4T No 1226, restored as MR No 6.

Unfortunately the idea was abandoned in 1932, as already recounted; the single wheeler was spared, but the others were ruthlessly cut up.

A fifth engine which had joined this collection was North London 4-4-0T, LMS 6445, previously NLR No 5 and LNWR No 2805. Built in 1894, and withdrawn in 1929, one of the last of its type to remain in traffic. This one never got as far as the restoration stage, and like the others was liquidated in 1932.

(Opposite above) Great Northern Stirling single No 1, which had not worked since 1907, being stored for many years in King's Cross shed and later placed in York Museum, from whence it was brought out and steamed again, thanks to the enterprise of the LNER. It ran on several public excursions, and one privately organised by the Railway Correspondence & Travel Society, between King's Cross and Peterborough or Cambridge, with a train of restored 'period' six-wheeled coaches. Seen here at Huntingdon on 11 September 1938 during a pause to take water.

One concludes by expressing the hope that in the not too distant future the present attitude of British Railways will be modified and that the powers that be will come to appreciate the great possibilities of running such excursions which would undoubtedly be of tremendous popularity, with much incidental publicity value.

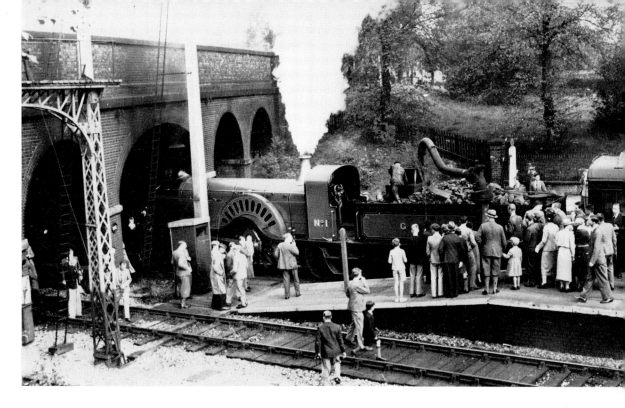

From Peace to War

General evacuation of children from London and other parts of the country in anticipation of massive air raids, which did not in fact materialise for many months. A scene at an unspecified station, between 1 and 4 September 1939, during which time 3,823 trains, carrying over a quarter of a million women and children, were sent away from London and other population centres such as Glasgow, Manchester, Merseyside, Tyneside to country areas.

Bibliography

Railway Magazine—Various issues
Railway Handbook—various issues
Railway Observer—various issues
The LMSR—Hamilton Ellis
History of the Southern Railway—Dendy-Marshall
Great Western Railway—McDermott

also many other publications to which sundry reference has had to be made, too numerous to list in detail.

Acknowledgements

Once again I have to express my thanks to Mr C. R. Clinker for reading through the main part of my manuscript, pages 7-27, also Appendix 2, and putting forward several suggestions for improvement, also ensuring the high standard of accuracy for which he is well known.

I must also place on record my appreciation of the help received from Mr T. J. Edgington, of BR Publicity, Euston, for sundry information, and also the supply of certain illustrations, in respect of which Mr N. W. Sprinks, in a similar capacity at Paddington, has also been most helpful. My son, Mr R. M. Casserley, was again able to make several useful suggestions, and to supply much of the information regarding coaching stock, of which he has made a special study.

Last, but not least, to my wife, for her valiant efforts in sorting out my own particular brand of 'shorthand', which she describes perhaps more accurately as just 'plain shocking handwriting' with its numerous alterations and additions caused by second and third thoughts.

Illustrations

BR Publicity, Euston
Pages 37, 41 (bottom), 42 (top), 44 (both), 45 (top), 94 (top), 99 (bottom), 108, 109 (bottom), 117 (all), 121 (top), 123 (bottom), 124
BR Publicity, Paddington
53 (both), 107 (top), 110 (top), 112 (bottom)
Courtesy A. Dunbar
35 (top)
Courtesy W. B. Yeadon
47 (top)

Most of the remaining illustrations are of the author's own taking. If any donor of photographs has been inadvertently omitted from the above list, the author proffers his apologies. The coloured plate and jacket cover depicting a train on the Oban line in 1927 is from a painting by Mr Victor Welch.

Index